Brimming with creative inspiration, how-to projects and useful information to enrich your everyday life, Quarto Knows is a favourite destination for those pursuing their interests and passions. Visit our site and dig deeper with our books into your area of interest: Quarto Creates, Quarto Cooks, Quarto Homes, Quarto Lives, Quarto Drives, Quarto Explores, Quarto Gifts, or Quarto Kids.

First published in the UK in 2019 by White Lion Publishing
an imprint of The Quarto Group
The Old Brewery, 6 Blundell Street
London N7 9BH
United Kingdom

www.QuartoKnows.com

First published in Spanish in 2017 by Lunwerg

© 2019 Quarto Publishing plc.
Text © 2017, 2018 Ivan Tapia

Ivan Tapia has asserted his moral right to be identified as the Author of this Work in accordance with the Copyright Designs and Patents Act 1988.

All rights reserved. No part of this book may be reproduced or utilised in any form or by any means, electronic or mechanical, including photocopying, recording or by any information storage and retrieval system, without permission in writing from White Lion Publishing.

Every effort has been made to trace the copyright holders of material quoted in this book. If application is made in writing to the publisher, any omissions will be included in future editions.

A catalogue record for this book is available from the British Library.

ISBN 978 1 78131 952 9
Ebook ISBN 978 1 78131 953 6

1 3 5 7 9 10 8 6 4 2
2019 2021 2023 2022 2020

Typeset in ITC New Baskerville
Illustrations and Design by Run Design

Printed in China

Publisher: Kerry Enzor
Editorial Director: Jennifer Barr
Proofreader: Katie Crous
Editorial Assistant: Bella Skertchly
Translators: Jackie Strachan and Jane Moseley
Art Director: Paileen Currie
Design: Dave Jones
Production Manager: Maeve Healy

ESCAPE BOOK 2

The Invisible Threat

Ivan Tapia

Montse Linde

WHITE LION PUBLISHING

READ THIS FIRST

In an escape book, the reader is the main character. The chapters are in the wrong order and you have to solve the puzzles one by one to find out where to continue reading.

If you enjoyed the first *Escape Book*, all about the Wanstein Club, you'll see that this second volume in the series contains lots of new elements to make the experience even more exciting.

How do I play along with this book?
Read each chapter until you come to the next padlock symbol:

Once there, just like Candela and Janina, the main characters in *Escape Book 2*, you have to go back and solve the puzzles that appear in the chapter to find out at which point you can take up the story again.

How do I solve and interpret the puzzles?
Your mission is to discover what lies behind each puzzle. A puzzle may reveal a number, the page you should turn to, or a word. If it is a word, then you need to discover how to convert it into a number in order to find out where to continue reading. The following clues will help you solve the puzzles:

A map: You will find a map behind the flaps of this book. In some puzzles you will need to use it to find the key.

The text: You will sometimes find keys or clues in the story itself to help you to decipher the puzzles. Read carefully!

Images in the text: Sometimes the characters find 'pieces'. Keep them handy, as they can be useful. But be careful: even if you find a piece of paper, it doesn't mean you need to use it immediately.

Puzzles: Full-page pictures which contain a puzzle that you must solve before you can continue reading.

To solve some of the puzzles you will have to interact with the drawing. If you don't want to do this on the book itself, make a copy of the pages or download them from the website address given on the final page of the chapter in question.

What happens if I can't solve the puzzles?

Don't worry. At the end of each chapter is the number of a page where you can find clues that will help you to achieve your goal.

It's up to you to decide whether you want to use just one clue, all the clues or no clues at all. *You* decide the level of difficulty of this book.

I hope that you can escape from this book along with Candela and Janina.

Good luck!

THE BEGINNING

A week ago, Candela received a map. On the back was the following message:

Candela spent several hours thinking about the offer and weighing it up, but finally decided not to accept it and put the map away in a box. Until today. It only takes a split-second to turn what was unthinkable a week ago into the only choice now.

Yes, she will accept their help now.

But first, she must find them.

TICK-TOCK TICK-TOCK TICK-TOCK TICK-TOCK

You haven't solved the puzzle on this page yet.
Find the code to work out where to continue reading.

If you need to, you can use the clues on page 162.

Write the code here so you can remember and refer to it later.

9

YOU HAVE SOLVED THE PUZZLE OF THE FIRST STEP

Continued from page 139.

THE DECISION

'Yes, yes, yes! That's the key, Candela, for sure!'

Janina claps her hands. Candela has to bite her lip in order not to tell her friend to shut up. She knows Janina is not to blame. It's her own fault: Candela confesses to herself that she barely has the patience to put up with all the excess energy of the people around her. There was another Candela before the Daedalus, but that Candela no longer exists.

'Why don't you enter the key straight away?'

'Because, if I do, I will break the promise I made to myself never to get into something like this again,' Candela thinks to herself. However, she can't tell Janina, so she says nothing.

Candela knows that the countdown will begin as soon as she enters the key and presses the button, and that there is no turning back. It is clearly stated on the Orwellians' website. 1,984 minutes. About 33 hours. But they tried to kill the boss and she can't let that go. *'It can't be worse than the Daedalus,'* she thinks. *'If I can get through this it will be worth it. Or will it?'*

She looks at Janina. She cannot confess that she is afraid because she doesn't know the price they'll have to pay… No, she can't say that. Now that Janina is convinced, this is no time to turn back. *'Or is it? What right have I got to get Janina involved in this mess?'*

Candela closes her eyes and sees the face of Castian Warnes, leader of the Wanstein Club, the man who nearly killed her in the Daedalus.

She hands Janina a pencil and a notebook.

'Take this down, Janina: mobile phone with really wide coverage, chargers, thermal blanket, pliers… Also water, energy bars, a pair of gloves, a torch…'

'Candela, are you dictating a shopping list to me?'

'Do you want to do this, Janina? You do? Well then, let's do it properly. I'm not letting you into this without even the most basic supplies.'

'But, why not...?'

'I'm not going to argue about this with you, Janina. I'm in charge here. Sorry, but that's the way it is. You'll be my eyes, my body, but I'm the one who thinks and takes the decisions. Take it or leave it. No sweat. If you're not sure, now's the time to say so.'

Candela holds her breath. She wants to do it, but part of her also wants Janina to give up, not to go down this path from which there is no return. To save herself now, while there is still time.

Janina looks at her, perplexed. She doesn't understand why Candela is talking to her in this way.

'How can I give up? Take a look at yourself, you can't do this on your own.'

That hurt, but Janina is right. *'I can't do it on my own.'* Candela has no need to look at herself. She knows what's what. She knew when she threw her high heels in the bin. She could no longer walk in them, it's hard enough getting about in trainers. She knew when she opened the wardrobe where she kept all her party clothes and packed them all up for the charity shop. All she kept was the green skirt and the battered blouse she was wearing when she got out of the Daedalus. She had pinned them to the living-room wall to remind herself that her war would not be over until she had destroyed Castian Warnes, the biggest son-of-a-bitch on the face of the Earth.

'I know, Janina. I know I can't do it. But that changes nothing. I'm going to be in charge of whatever we do. I'll take the decisions and you'd better obey. That's the only way I can protect you. And if you don't think you can do it that way, you'd better tell me right now because, once you start, there'll be no turning back. So I ask you again: are you sure you want to do this?'

'I owe it to him.'

That is a reason she understands perfectly. Candela owes it

12

to him too. He has always been there, he's always had her back. Though she wonders whether he might be just an excuse to do what she was going to do anyway. *'May you forgive me,'* she thinks to herself.

'OK, then. Carry on noting this down…'

By the time Candela finishes dictating, Janina's list covers over a page. She takes the credit card Candela holds out to her, and asks:

'When are you going to enter the key?'

'Once you are in London. Get everything I told you, rest up for a while and I'll take you to the airport first thing tomorrow morning.'

London. The city in which Orwell's novel is set, and also the city on the map sent to Candela a week ago. So, following her instinct, she sent Janina there before entering the key. Once the clock starts, the countdown will continue relentlessly, and they can't afford to waste a single second.

She leaves Janina at the airport as the sun began to rise. Then she goes to the hospital, where she tries to get some sleep in the room where the boss had been admitted. She needs a clear head for the next few hours.

She turns on the computer – the Orwellians' website is open and the phone fully charged. Everything is ready for Janina's call.

The mobile phone rings. JANINA. She lets it ring four times. There's still time to stop this madness. Or is there? Perhaps she lost her marbles ages ago. She glances over at the boss. *I'm sorry,'* she says silently. Then she presses the green button to answer Janina's call.

'Candela, I'm here. Where do I go?'

'Just a second, Janina, I'm going to enter the key.'

Typing. A click. OK.

One second. Two seconds. The website loads and everything begins.

The stopwatch starts up, and Candela synchronises it with her watch.

'Janina? I'll read you what it says.

'You have 1,984 minutes to reach Goldstein. To do so, you'll have to get past all of Big Brother's tricks and lies:

The Ministry of Truth,

The Ministry of Plenty,

The Ministry of Peace,

The Ministry of Love

and
Room 101.

You will only see the truth if you can get into and escape from Room 101.'

Candela has read the book and knows all the horrors that lie behind each ministry, not to mention the torture that is inflicted in 101, where the worst nightmares become reality. But there is no going back now.

'Candela, are you still there?'

'Yes, Janina, I'm trying to solve the puzzle that will lead us to the first challenge, the Ministry of Truth.'

Candela observes the characters that start to appear on the computer screen.

TICK-TOCK TICK-TOCK TICK-TOCK TICK-TOCK

```
        4 4 5 5 3 4 7 1
        3 4 T H E 4 5 8
        8 8 2 3 9 1 7 0
        0 0 1 3 8 2 1 3
        6 C I R C L E 0
        6 2 7 8 2 3 4 9
        1 9 2 3 9 8 1 3
        9 8 5 8 9 8 1 2
4 5 5 3 4 5 8 3 4 5 8 3 4 5 8 8
3 9 1 7 0 0 M A R K S 3 6 1 4 4
2 7 8 2 3 4 9 1 9 2 3 9 8 1 3 9
8 9 8 1 2 7 3 7 7 4 6 8 2 3 4 0
5 2 3 0 4 9 8 5 8 8 2 3 4 4 7 6
1 2 8 5 9 5 9 9 6 8 3 4 5 8 9 9
        4 4 5 5 3 4 5 8
        3 4 T H E 4 5 8
        8 8 2 3 9 1 7 0
        0 0 1 3 8 2 1 3
        6 1 4 4 4 1 6 2
        7 8 P L A C E 9
        2 3 9 8 1 3 9 8
        5 8 9 8 1 2 7 3
```

You haven't solved the puzzle on this page yet.
Find the code to work out where to continue reading.

If you need to, you can use the clues on page 162.

Write the code here so you can remember and refer to it later.

17

YOU HAVE SOLVED THE PUZZLE OF THE ENTRANCE TO THE MINISTRY OF TRUTH

Continued from page 124.

18

THE DOOR OF TRUTH

The trapdoor opens. There is no longer any doubt. A staircase descends into a darkness so thick she cannot see where it ends.

'Do you really want me to go down there?'

'There's no choice, Janina.'

'I can go back the way I came.'

'Giving up so soon? Trust me, I won't let anything happen to you.'

'What about the boss? How is he?'

'No change.'

Candela can hear Janina's breathing over the microphone and sense her fear, but the young woman takes the plunge anyway. Cautiously Janina descends the steps, focusing the camera on everything around her: floor, blue Orwellian symbol, left-hand wall, ceiling, right-hand wall, step… Floor, Orwellian symbol, left-hand wall, ceiling, right-hand wall, step… Floor, left-hand wall, ceiling, right-hand wall, step…

'That's great, Janina, you're doing really well. Go on, one more step.'

'When she gets to the bottom of the steps, Candela estimates that she has gone down three or four storeys and is under the streets of London.

'Can you see anything?'

'Nothing.'

'What does it smell of, Janina?'

'Of damp.'

'Can you hear anything?'

'Silence, too much silence, to tell the truth.'

'Well, go on then, keep walking.'

Candela does not like what Janina said about the silence, not one bit. It's not normal to hear nothing at all in an underground gallery. There is always something: air seeping in somewhere, creaking noises, the odd rodent... Candela knows they are not alone. *'Come on, Janina, love, you can do it,'* she thinks to herself.

Janina whistles a song by The Cure, the boss's favourite group, now also hers. Trying to block out what is around her. Then, when she enters the tunnel before her, a string of little lamps come on to light up her way forward. She gasps involuntarily.

Click!

The trapdoor she used to enter from the library snaps shut.

'That was the wind, wasn't it, Candela? Tell me it was. Luckily I kept the key in my backpack.'

Candela does not share her certainty that the wind had nothing to do with it. Nor that she doubts that the key Janina kept will be useful.

'What are you doing, Janina? Where are you going?'

'To check whether I can open the trapdoor.'

'No, Janina, there's no time to waste. We don't know how many tests are left.'

'...'

'Janina!'

But Janina is already back at the top of the steps. There is no keyhole on her side. The trapdoor is locked.

'I'm locked in!' Her voice betrays more surprise than fear.

'Calm down. And don't disobey me again, Janina.'

'Calm down? Get lost! They've locked me in down here and all you do is tell me off like a little girl. I'm the one trapped in a tunnel full of mould and God knows what else.'

'I know. I realise you're the one locked in, not me, and believe me, I'm sorry. But we've just started out, and I'm not going to

20

argue about every decision. You can't get out. And you won't be able to get out, at least until we solve the puzzle of the Ministry of Truth. You knew what you were getting into, so grow up and get moving.'

It was a harsh way to treat Janina, but she couldn't allow panic to set in. She needs her to be strong and alert.

Janina does not answer; her silence does the talking. Without a word, she retraces her steps down once more. She turns the camera in a full circle so that Candela can see everything too.

'Good.'

Despite her anger, Janina knows that Candela is her only hope of getting out of this mess. And Candela can tell that *she* is angry because she's not moving so slowly now. She's moving much faster.

'Good, good, we're doing well.'

TICK-TOCK TICK-TOCK TICK-TOCK TICK-TOCK

The tunnel is longer than Janina expected. It takes about fifteen minutes to get to the end and she dislikes being locked in.

They found nothing along the way, apart from another three Orwellian symbols: two on the right followed by one on the left.

'Candela, I've just reached the Ministry of Truth,' Janina says, all trace of anger now gone from her voice.

'How do you know?'

'Because it says so.'

So it seems. Janina aims the camera carefully so that Candela can see a door, upon which is a kind of carved face.

'It's a copy of the "Mouth of Truth" in Rome,' says Janina.

She knows, because barely a week ago she had watched *Roman Holiday* with the boss. A cigarette between his lips, he had made her laugh by claiming that he looked just like Gregory Peck. According to the film, if a liar puts their hand inside the Mouth of Truth, they will lose it.

21

The inscription over the stone mouth reads:

He who tells the truth shall live without fear.

'Did you see the words, Candela?'

'Yes, I think they want you to put your hand in.'

Janina doesn't move.

'Janina, you have to put your hand in – there's no time to waste.'

'I'm afraid of rats.'

'But there are no rats there.'

'There are usually rats in underground holes.'

'Alright, listen to me. Put the mobile as close as you can to the opening and I'll check, and when I say "Now!", you put your hand straight in. I'm sure there are no rats in there. OK?'

Candela knows that it's unlikely any good will come of it, but she also knows that the people who thought all this up won't let the 'game' end so quickly.

'Now!!!'

Both girls hear the *click* as the stone mouth closes tightly around Janina's wrist. She goes crazy. All that wasted energy doesn't help anyone, but she can't stop herself. Candela lets her scream, kick and swear as much as she wants for a few seconds.

'Calm down, Janina, calm down! If you don't stop twisting and fighting, you'll lose your hand. And we need you in one piece. There's still a long way to go.'

'A long way to go, Candela? What the hell have you let me in for? You told me we had to reach the Orwellians, that they were the only ones who could stop that creep Castian who tried to kill the boss! They're supposed to be the good guys, aren't they?'

'They can help us, Janina, believe me.'

Fortunately, Janina can't see how Candela tightens her fists until her knuckles go white. The journalist speaks calmly and gently:

22

'We'll find a way to get your hand out... Hey, show me the inscription again! It's changed, hasn't it? You must have set off a mechanism when you put your hand in.'

Answer the question and tell the truth. If not, you will lose your hand.

'They're going to cut my hand off, Candela! These guys are crazy. Call the police, for God's sake!'

'Easy, Janina, nobody is going to cut your hand off. Give me just a second.'

Candela closes her eyes. She counts to ten. She concentrates for a moment, then breathes out and opens her eyes again. A little calmer now, Janina points the camera at the door. It is covered in Orwellian symbols. The solution must be staring them in the face.

In the novel *1984*, Public Enemy Number One was Big Brother, the focal point of all the tests and tortures that Winston, the main character, was subjected to. The Ministry of Truth changed history, distorted the truth...

'Remember the symbols, Janina. Calm down and remember them.'

'...'

'Janina, I'm going to get you out, I promise. Calm down. They're playing with our fear. They want us to lose control of ourselves, but we won't give them that pleasure. Keep on pointing the camera.'

TICK-TOCK TICK-TOCK TICK-TOCK TICK-TOCK

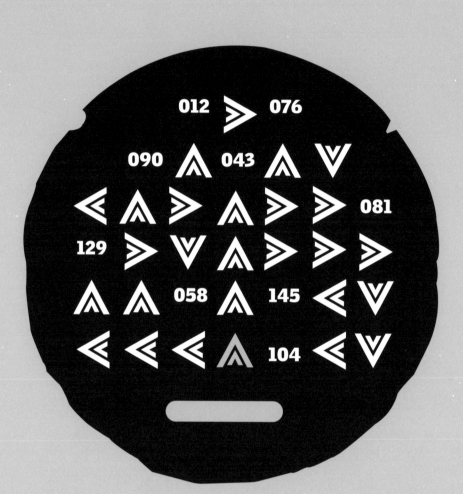

You haven't solved the puzzle on this page yet.
Find the code to work out where to continue reading.

If you need to, you can use the clues on page 162.

Write the code here so you can remember and refer to it later.

YOU HAVE SOLVED THE PUZZLE OF THE SECOND NEXUS

Continued from page 118.

From what they were able to learn in the Nexus Room, it seems their next goal is the Ministry of Peace, housed in Fort Grain on the Thames estuary. Built in 1855 to protect the English coast, the fort survived bombing during two world wars, and today is abandoned. There is only one problem: from St Dunstan to Fort Grain is about fourteen hours on foot. Candela doubts whether Janina will make it. She is very tired, and they don't know whether the gas she inhaled was a narcotic, or something worse.

They are running out of time. According to her calculations, by the time Janina arrives they will have less than ten hours left to reach and solve the puzzles at the Ministry of Peace, the Ministry of Love and Room 101. Not to mention the fact that Janina really needs a few hours' sleep. It is impossible. Candela is in despair. But there is no choice but to keep going.

Janina refused to take a rest. Since Candela told her that the boss might wake up soon, she has felt full of renewed energy. The journalist does not want to think about what will happen when Janina finds out the truth: the doctor has informed her that the boss has just hours to live.

Candela is incandescent with rage. She needs some fresh air. She goes down to have something to eat in the hospital café. She orders a still water and a few bread sticks. She takes her snack to the lift and goes back to keep watch over the man who has been such a pillar for her recently. Going past the newsstand she sees the cover of a sensationalist magazine with a headline about the Orwellians:

The column supporting the well-known Angel of Peace in Munich has been covered in camouflage gear in a clear reference to war. Sewn into the fabric used are photos of the leaders of several Western countries that maintain trade relations with the key arms producers [...]

Candela has been convinced for some time that an extremely powerful person is pulling the strings behind this group. It's the only possible explanation. It would be practically impossible to carry out all those stunts unless someone was turning a blind eye. We live in a world in which our every move is recorded: via bank cards, video cameras, mobile phones... The Orwellians have not been caught because someone doesn't want them to be caught.

Candela pulls the boss's blanket up to keep him warm. Suddenly she feels cold. Or perhaps she is shivering because she realises that what she is doing to Janina isn't much better than what they did to her. She's using Janina, forcing the girl to do her will. But there is no turning back now.

'*I have to do it,*' Candela reassures herself. If they can get through all this, Candela will be able to sink Castian forever. That is the only thing that matters to her now.

So she turns on her computer and watches as the red dot advances through the maze of tunnels under London.

TICK-TOCK TICK-TOCK TICK-TOCK TICK-TOCK

Janina proceeds along her path. The landscape has changed. The tunnels she passed through before were like railway tunnels but without the rails. The walls were dirty, but they were built of brick. Now, the sides are formed by rough, bare rock. They are like the galleries in mines you see on television. As previously, she has asked Candela to leave her alone as she hikes along. The way she is feeling, if they ever speak to each other again it will be too soon.

Her body is tired but her mind is awake. Candela wanted her to sleep but she prefers to keep going: the sooner she gets there, the better. From time to time she allows herself to pause and rest for a few minutes. She feels trapped underground and all she wants to do is get out.

She thinks about everything that has happened. Obviously, the Orwellians are barking mad, but when she gets out of here she's going to read *1984* carefully. She is surprised that the world described in a book written in the 1940s could be so similar to the world today. The Ministry of Truth concerns itself with lies: '*That ministry exists today, too,*' Janina thinks to herself. Some of her friends were forced to go abroad to find work, and now it turns out that doing whatever you have to in order to make a life for yourself is known as 'external mobility'. Wage cuts are known as 'adjustments', and building a wall to separate the two Americas is 'security', not 'shame'. In *1984*, the Ministry of Abundance made sure that people kept their heads down and got on with their work, providing them with the bare minimum they needed to get by. *'Just like now, when we work like animals but stay poor.'*

According to what Candela has told her, the Ministry of Peace, the goal of her journey now, concerns itself with war. The ministry was constantly declaring war, first against one bloc and then the other. That helped them to keep people under control, ensuring they had no desire to travel and discover other cultures, and that they always thought the best thing that could happen to them was to have a leader like the one they had, a leader who defended them and kept them safe. *'Orwell must have been pretty smart. It's as if he could see the future,'* she thinks.

She has sent Candela a picture of the cube she found in the last hexagonal room. That makes two.

But Candela has said nothing as yet. When they next talk, Janina will ask her what she has been able to learn. She doesn't like being so dependent on Candela.

29

The path seems to be endless. She has been walking for six hours but feels as if she has got precisely nowhere. Not even halfway. Janina can't think clearly any more; in fact she isn't thinking at all. Her mind is blank as she places one foot in front of another. The rock chamber where she started out has turned into a kind of gallery, its walls painted white. And her path, once made of beaten earth, is now paved.

She knows she should stop, but she struggles on. Her eyes close. She's going to fall. She's going to hurt herself. From time to time, she sees huge letters on the walls. They are so big, so striking, she can hardly miss them. She has no idea what they mean, but she photographs them and sends them to Candela. By now, she realises that nothing she sees, hears or walks past is there by chance.

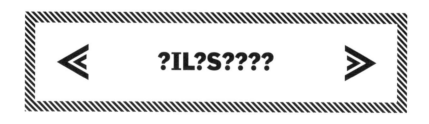

She can't go on. Her legs are weak. She finds a little sheltered place and sits down on the ground. She covers herself in her thermal blanket. It's getting cooler. She calls Candela.

'How is the boss? Has he woken up?'

'No, not yet. How are you?'

'Bad. I can't go on. I need to rest. How much time have we got left?'

'Sleep a bit and I'll wake you up.'

'Don't patronise me. I'm the one that's down here. I don't know who these guys are, but I'm pretty sure they'll stop at nothing.'

Candela does not reply. While Janina is angry with her, she won't ask too many questions. She lets the girl rest for a while.

Lying down on the floor with the strap of the backpack wrapped around her arm, it feels like months since she boarded that plane for London, yet she had landed only this morning.

When she got to the airport, she was dying to get justice for what had happened to the boss. Now, she's not even sure that what Candela says is true. Thousands of accidents like the one the boss was in happen every day. What reasons does Candela have to say it was attempted murder? Who cares. Only Candela and a group of crazy people know where she is. If anything happens to her, nobody is going to come and look for her. Nobody will care. The only one who *would* care is fighting for his life in hospital. Janina cries herself to sleep. She does not want to die.

814 minutes

Nearly four hours later, Candela saw that Janina was on the march once more. There had been no need to wake her. Candela is worried, because the clock is ticking and she does not know how much more time they will need to solve the tests that await them. There are another fourteen hours to go. After all she has put Janina through, it would be so unfair if they failed due to lack of time, but she knows that the rules are implacable. In the world in which they are now operating, no one will show any mercy.

TICK-TOCK TICK-TOCK TICK-TOCK TICK-TOCK

There were ever more forks along the tunnel that Janina is travelling along, forcing her to stop and check the map regularly. But Candela phoned her a short while ago and is now guiding her through these underground passages, allowing her no freedom to make her own decisions. 'Remember, I'm the one who thinks, I'm the one who decides,' Candela had insisted. And she is right. Janina might hate Candela, but the journalist is her only chance.

She doesn't know how many hours she has been walking, and prefers not to look at her watch. The walls on either side are getting damper and damper, and beginning to smell of the sea.

'That's because we are reaching the mouth of the Thames, where the fort is,' explains Candela.

To her right, she sees more letters like those she saw earlier. She takes a photo and sends it to Candela.

32

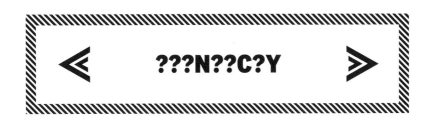

???N??C?Y

In less than an hour she reaches the Ministry of Peace, announced in metal letters on a door that looks like that of a safe. Janina knows what to look for. She stays completely calm. It's as if she had lost the ability to feel, like the zombies in those films she loves so much and which bore the boss to tears.

'I'm sending you the text, Candela':

For there to be peace, there must be war. That is the truth of Big Brother. Our mobile phones are made from war, our parties are made from war, our sleeping lives are made from war. Human progress gives life to some and death to others.

'*That is so* true,' thinks Janina. '*All those marches for peace and social justice, but we wear clothes made by children in India.*'

'Now, how do I open the door?'

'Have you tried turning the knob?'

Candela is only trying to lighten things up a bit, but, to the surprise of both of them, the door opens easily.

'I don't believe it!' says Janina, entering the room.

'No!!!'

Candela's yelled warning makes Janina jump back over the threshold again.

'It's a trap! Remember, things are never as simple as they seem. You see the light, which looks as if it is entering through a window? Well, there is no window.'

33

Janina takes a good look and sees a pattern of thin beams of light over the entrance.

'Candela, I can't move. More light beams have appeared behind me, about two metres away. And they're coming closer.'

While Candela tries to think how to get her out of there, Janina's imagination runs wild. *'It must be some kind of laser beam that will slice me into pieces.'*

TICK-TOCK TICK-TOCK TICK-TOCK TICK-TOCK

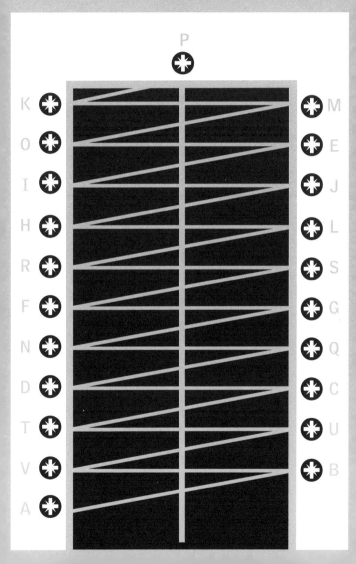

You haven't solved the puzzle on this page yet.
Find the code to work out where to continue reading.

If you need to, you can use the clues on page 162.

Write the code here so you can remember and refer to it later.

36

YOU HAVE SOLVED THE PUZZLE OF THE THIRD NEXUS

Continued from page 144.

The next stop is the old Abney Park Cemetery in Stoke Newington, central London. Built as a burial place for Dissenters, Protestants who rejected the Anglican church, the cemetery was closed in the 1970s. They say that this is the most silent place in the city.

This is where we find the Ministry of Love and the last test before reaching Room 101. But Candela knows it is practically impossible to resolve the puzzle before time runs out. They only have five hours left, and Abney Park Cemetery is fourteen hours away. Then there is the time they will need to solve the puzzles.

But they won't give up, they'll keep on fighting until the last second has elapsed. Having solved the problem of the airlock without Candela's help, Janina feels more sure of herself. Candela watches the red dot advance apparently unstoppably across the screen. It reminds her of the girl she herself once was: strong, confident, scared of nothing – well, not much, anyway. Only what you really needed to be scared of.

But sometimes things happen and you can't do anything about it. The boss just died. The machines started beeping, an army of doctors and nurses rushed into the room and it was all over. He didn't even open his eyes to say goodbye to her. For the best, perhaps; it would have been unbearable.

She decides not to tell Janina though – that news can wait until she gets out. She doesn't want the girl to lose momentum – that's all they've got left right now. Candela certainly believes her friend is brave. She looks at the map again. Perhaps… The phone rings.

'Hello, has the boss woken up yet?'

'No, Janina, I'm sorry, not yet... At this rate, we won't get there in time. Do you think you could run a bit more? About a kilometre from where you are is an area where they did some construction a few years ago. They used lorries to transport the building material. Perhaps something is still there.'

Ten minutes later, Janina reaches the spot they were talking about, and informs Candela that she can't see anything that could be used for transport – there's only one tunnel wider than the others and some rails.

'What rails, Janina?'

'Railway lines.'

'Railway lines?'

'Yes.'

'...'

'There's one of those old wagons they use to carry heavy loads.'

'We have to start it up, Janina.'

'I can't. I think it's a puzzle. Below the ignition switches are some letters like the ones I showed you before.

Candela looks, then smiles. If she's right, then the game is not over, not yet.

TICK-TOCK TICK-TOCK TICK-TOCK TICK-TOCK

Z????H?H?

You haven't solved the puzzle on this page yet.
Find the code to work out where to continue reading.

If you need to, look at the clues on pages 162–163.

Write the code here so you can remember and refer to it later.

41

YOU HAVE SOLVED THE PUZZLE OF THE GRAVESTONE

Continued from page 129.

14 minutes

Once she manages to move the stone, Candela finds a kind of spiral ramp. The entrance. *'A helter-skelter! Considering I can hardly walk, that's really cool!'* she thinks, ironically. She has no idea where it will take her, but she knows this is her only chance of reaching Janina. It's a one-way journey. There will be no turning back.

So she slides down, round and round, for about thirty metres, until the ramp comes to a sudden end, with still some distance to the ground. She jumps, tumbling to the ground. The shock of the fall leaves her gasping, but there is nothing broken.

She now finds herself in a narrow corridor with a door at each end. The door to the left must be the bottom of the coffin. It's open on this side. *'That means Janina got out. Where are you?'* she thinks.

The door on the right is made of metal and has metal numbers on it: 101. They have reached the final puzzle and no doubt the hardest, too. Perhaps she'll never get out of this, but she's no longer scared. She just wants to get it over with. *'You wanna fight? Well, here I am!'*

Reaching the door, she sees a simple numerical keypad. She taps in 101. Nothing happens. *'Well, I had to try,'* she thinks. In the shadows, she sees Janina's backpack.

'Oh no! They've got her! Janinaaaaa!!!' she screams as loudly as she can, but no reply comes.

Then, behind her, she hears a slight sound, a click, and looking towards where the sound came from, she sees rats falling through the hole she used to enter this place. One, two, three... By the

43

way they bare their teeth, there is no doubt that they are hungry. At the rate they are falling, there'll soon be too many. She needs to act quickly. She must find Janina now, so she can waste no time feeling sorry for herself. There are more and more rats, and they are starting to make quite a din. They know; they know that Janina is terrified of rats. She doesn't want to think about how her friend must have screamed if she had to go through this. It pains her. Because of the novel, Candela knew that sooner or later these animals would appear, but she did not tell her friend. Just as she has not told Janina many other things. *'I'm sorry, I'm really sorry, Janina.'*

Candela takes a look around. Door, wall, door, bone, wall, ceiling, backpack, floor, rats, tube… She sniffs the air. Door, wall, door, bone, wall, ceiling, backpack, floor, rats, tube… The clock continues to tick relentlessly.

Then she sees it. Where else? On the door of Room 101.

TICK-TOCK TICK-TOCK TICK-TOCK TICK-TOCK

44

What is hidden is not unknown to you

You haven't solved the puzzle on this page yet.
Find the code to work out where to continue reading.

If you need to, you can use the clues on page 163.

Write the code here so you can remember and refer to it later.

46

YOU HAVE SOLVED
THE GOLDSTEIN PUZZLE

Continued from page 113.

ORWELLIANS ATTACK AGAIN

Yesterday afternoon, the magnate Castian Warnes died in a bomb attack in London. He will be given a state funeral. All Europe mourns his loss.

www.cocolisto.com/ukeb2

YOU HAVE SOLVED THE PUZZLE OF THE RAILS

Continued from page 41.

264
minutes

Janina is rattling along in a wagon beneath the largest city in the European Union. Candela has informed her that she will reach her destination in four hours. She is just glad not to have to walk. She has blisters on her feet already and knows she is reaching the limits of her strength. *'I'll get out somehow. I'm not giving up,'* she says to herself as she bandages her wounds. When she gets out, she'll ask the police to conduct a thorough investigation into the boss's accident. And she will blow the whistle on Candela if she finds out the journalist lied to her and deliberately put her life in danger.

TICK-TOCK TICK-TOCK TICK-TOCK TICK-TOCK

While Janina rolls along underground, Candela goes over the story of Winston and Julia once more. In Orwell's novel, they fall in love and conduct their affair clandestinely for as long as they can. They know that one day they will be found out and punished. They promise not to betray each other. The methods used by the ministry are 'highly persuasive', and they may give each other away. But that does not matter: their triumph lies in their continuing love for each other. Unfortunately, however, their love cannot withstand the torture they are subjected to in Room 101. Candela does not want to even think about what is in store for Janina.

Truth – Lies
Plenty – Scarcity
Peace – War

50

Love… It can only be Hate

As Janina's wagon whisks her along the tracks, Candela gently closes the eyes of her most loyal friend and accompanies him to the hospital morgue. 'Goodbye, boss. I'm sorry,' she says, kissing him.

Then she buys a ticket on the first plane to London. Hopefully, she'll arrive a few minutes before Janina reaches Abney Park Cemetery. She just hopes that nothing bad happens to Janina while she is offline.

TICK-TOCK TICK-TOCK TICK-TOCK TICK-TOCK

Over the space of four hours, one travelling underground, the other by air, the two of them come closer and closer to their destinations.

TICK-TOCK TICK-TOCK TICK-TOCK TICK-TOCK

Candela has landed in London. For the last few seconds, she has been breathing in the quiet of Abney Park. Her gaze is fixed on the tracker on her mobile phone. At last, the red dot has reached the cemetery, where they hope to find the entrance to the Ministry of Love. Janina is under her very feet right now. Just a few metres of earth separate them, but Candela decides not to tell her friend for the moment. To give her that information would also confirm to her that the boss is dead.

Janina is now travelling along a tunnel that might have been drilled straight through the earth. It smells of damp and the air is fusty. She shivers from the cold. Not even the thermal blanket over her shoulders provides any warmth. And being in a cemetery is no joke.

When she was little, they used to play at telling horror stories. 'Did you know that there are people who wake up inside their coffins after they have been buried? My uncle worked at the cemetery and he says that you can hear desperate screams at night, and that in the morning the earth has clearly been disturbed...' She had never thought that telling horror stories was much fun. No one ever came to rescue her when she was having her worst nightmares, scrabbling away at the earth to try to get out of the grave she had been lowered into.

When the wagon comes to a halt, she phones Candela.

'I'm nearly there. I'll show you everything I can see on the screen, OK?' she says as she continues to walk.

Candela moves along exactly in step with Janina, making sure she is always exactly above her young friend underground. She is dressed in black: black trousers, black pullover, black trainers. And a leather jacket that is too big for her, since it used to belong to the boss.

'This is ghastly, Candela. These people leave their dead lying around on the floor. It's full of bones...'

'Janina?'

'...'

'Janina?'

'I can hear music.'

Janina stops and listens hard. She hears the strains of 'End Love' by OK Go, which she recognises because he had recently seen the music video.

'That song's really out of place here,' says Janina.

As she approaches the wall before her, the music gets louder, as if each step increases the volume by one decibel.

'Janina, stop just a second!' Candela shouts to make herself heard. 'As you go forward, the volume goes up, and soon we won't be able to hear each other. If you need to tell me something, you'll have to go back until I can hear you. Do you understand me?'

'Yes. I can see something that looks like a door. I'll go and have a look, come back and tell you about it.'

52

'OK, I'll wait. Be careful!'

Candela looks at her watch. Twenty-nine minutes and thirty seconds and it will all be over.

Had she not known full well that these guys don't mess around, Janina would describe what she sees as a joke in the worst possible taste. This time, instead of a door, an upright coffin stands before her. To dispel any doubts, a sign announces the entrance to the Ministry of Love.

Before she goes back to report to Candela, she tries to move the coffin. Impossible. She can't. It is tightly attached to the wall. A wooden engraving announces that Winston and Julia are buried here. She opens the lid and... God, how disgusting! She runs back to tell Candela what she has just seen.

'What took so long? Time's running out.'

'The door is Julia and Winston's coffin... It's attached to the wall, but inside... there's just one skeleton with its arms spread out as if it wants to hug someone. It's disgusting... I took some photos. I can't stand this. I'm sending them to you... I...'

'Concentrate, Janina, take a deep breath and concentrate. Are you sure it said *Winston and Julia*?'

'Yes, I'm sure. What's the surprise?'

'No surprise. Winston and Julia are the lovers in *1984*.'

'Can you think of anything?' Janina asks her.

'Yes, but you're not going to like it. I think you have to shake the skeleton's hand.'

'I'm not doing it! No way am I shaking that bloody skeleton's hand. I just won't! Get it? Do you understand?' Janina screams into the void.

'Calm down, I don't think it is even a real skeleton. But I'm afraid you'll have to if we're going to get out of this alive.'

'You come and do it if you want, but I am not touching those bones! How low am I supposed to sink? And do me a favour. Stop saying "we", in the plural. I'm the only one who is stuck in a cemetery and can't get out.'

Candela knows that the puzzle of the Ministry of Love is only just beginning. And she feels so sorry for Janina.

'Stop behaving like a child! Go and touch it! Go on!'

Janina stamps her foot. 'No, I won't!' But she knows she has no choice. As a child, she learned that no one was going to help her. So she sips some water from her bottle and goes back. Staring at the plaque that reads MINISTRY OF LOVE, and without looking at the skeleton, she takes what must once have been a hand and immediately feels a slight electric shock, a tingling in her hand. Surprised, she turns her gaze on the skull before her and sees that its eye sockets are illuminated by a dim light. She screams and takes a step back.

She's panting so much she can hardly breathe. If she doesn't get a grip on herself she'll have a panic attack, and this is not the best place for it, so she tries to calm down and think clearly. She'll do what she has been doing for the last few hours. Get by as best she can. She goes back to the coffin, grips the bones of the hand again, puts up with the electric shock until she has filmed everything, then sends the results to Candela. OK Go's 'End Love' continues to play.

'Yes, I think there's something in its eyes,' says Candela, 'but there isn't enough light. Janina, I want you to know that you've been very brave and I'm so sorry you have to go through all this…'

'Shut up, Candela. Don't try to butter me up. Just tell me what it is you want me to do.'

'OK. Go back and embrace it. That's what Julia would do to Winston. We need the eyes to light up more powerfully if we are going to open the door. The harder you embrace it, the more light we will have, I'm guessing. So get over there. We have very little time left.'

'What will happen if the time runs out?'

'I have no idea, but we'd better not waste any time thinking about it. Get over there now!'

54

Candela looks at her watch again. *'Don't fail me now, Janina, not now.'*

No thinking. Candela cannot allow Janina to ask questions, that would be the end. She knows full well what will happen if the time runs out before they solve Room 101.

Janina embraces the skeleton, and the coffin door closes. She shouts out, screams with all her might, but she knows that Candela cannot hear her. The electric shock she receives becomes increasingly strong. There is no space, the music is deafening. She can't even get out of her embrace with that bundle of bones... She's going to die, she's going to die like she does in her worst nightmares. Yes, she's going to die buried under a cemetery... The electric shocks hurt... She feels so powerless, her lungs are bursting.

'Help!!!'

Behind Janina, engraved on the coffin lid, is a text. She cannot see it:

Torture will purify your soul.

She grits her teeth and forces herself to look into the eye sockets of the skull two centimetres from her mouth. She reads what she sees there. Good thing she saw the music video of the song recently.

TICK-TOCK TICK-TOCK TICK-TOCK TICK-TOCK

OyuUbet: KO Og Den Ovel

You haven't solved the puzzle on this page yet.
Find the code to work out where to continue reading.

If you need to, you can use the clues on page 163.

Write the code here so you can remember and refer to it later.

YOU HAVE SOLVED THE PUZZLE OF THE GATE OF PEACE

Continued from page 36.

Candela is completely confused. The letters that Janina photographed for her offer no help in solving this puzzle, so she files them next to the images of the cubes in the nexus rooms. She knows that there is nothing random in all of this, and that at some point, these images will provide the key that will enable them to advance.

'Go in.'

Janina tried to keep the door from closing. Impossible. She used all her strength, but could not prevent it from happening. *That's OK. What would I have ended up doing, anyway? Walking for another fourteen hours back to where I came from? No. There is only one way out and that's by moving forward,'* she thinks.

Click.

The room she is in now is a cistern built underground, a cubic tank measuring around three by three metres. In the ceiling, about three metres high, is a trapdoor. Embedded in the walls are several rectangular fish tanks, all the same size. She describes all of this to Candela while showing it to her on camera.

'There is one tank with orange fish, another with blue fish, another with black fish... Can you see all of this, Candela?'

'Are there the same number of fish in all the tanks? I can't count them from here.'

'No... I just checked that. And there are taps under some of the tanks.'

'What is on the other side?'

'On the opposite wall are vertical lines crossed by horizontal stripes with numbers written beside them. Like a ruler. And here on my left it says:

'If you are afraid of what is outside, you will remain locked inside.'

'OK, Janina. The ruler on the wall measures the height of the liquid when the tank is full. Now we just need to find out how to get to the trapdoor in the ceiling. Can you reach it somehow?'

'Impossible. But let me try something.'

Without hesitating, Janina turns on the tap below the tank that contains the blue fish. Cascading onto the floor, the water quickly covers her shoes, and goes up to her calves… The floodgates are really open now, and the water is rising fast. The young girl holds up her backpack and mobile phone to make sure they don't get wet, then takes out an airtight bag and puts both inside.

'Did I turn on the tap too soon?' she wonders. *'What if the water doesn't stop rising?'* She'll drown. Simple as that. She is under a defence tower on the River Thames.

On the other side of the chamber, Candela watches as all the water empties out of the fish tank.

At last, the water stops rising. The gauge on the wall shows a depth of around forty centimetres.

'OK. I'm not drowning yet. All the taps empty one fish tank,' says Janina. 'If I turn on another, the water will reach my waist, after the third I'll be swimming, and so on until I get to the exit door. I'm really sure about this, Candela.'

'Just a second, Janina. Let's not get ahead of ourselves here, it could be dangerous. After everything that's happened, do you really think it's going to be so easy?'

'Are you jealous, Candela? Are you jealous because I found out how to get out of here before you? What did that text say? *If you are afraid of what is outside, you will remain locked inside.* It's obvious what I need to do. Let the water in.'

60

'Don't be childish, Janina, you're much better than that.' She ponders the question for a while. 'Have you calculated the amount of water that will enter every time you turn on a tap? If the tank fills right up, then…'

'There's a good chance I'll drown.'

'Exactly.'

Although it's hard to admit, she must accept that if it weren't for Candela, she would already be dead.

'And how do I know which tap to turn on? One thing is certain – it's the only way to get to the door.'

'That's what we have to find out. But if we know that the tank measures about three by three by three metres, and there's about forty centimetres of water now, to get to the exit you still need another 21,000 litres or so.

TICK-TOCK TICK-TOCK TICK-TOCK TICK-TOCK

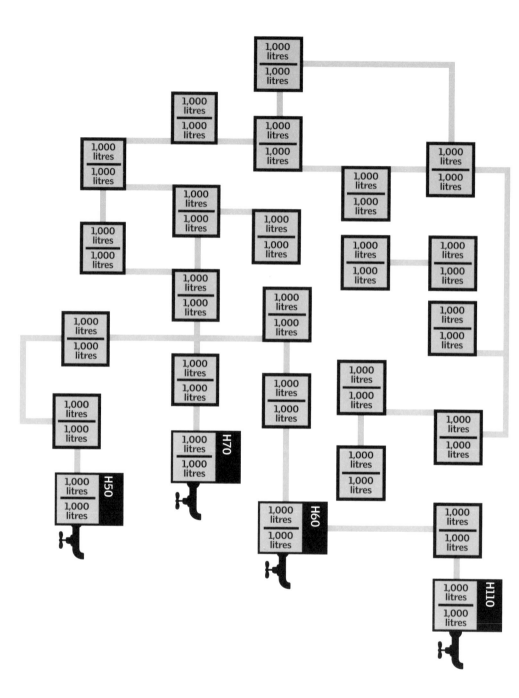

You haven't solved the puzzle on this page yet.
Find the code to work out where to continue reading.

If you need to, you can use the clues on page 163.

Write the code here so you can remember and refer to it later.

63

YOU HAVE SOLVED THE PUZZLE OF THE MINISTRY OF TRUTH

Continued from page 151.

Now Janina can't even stand in the room. She's about to be crushed to death between the ceiling and the floor. She is perspiring terribly. She never thought she could sweat so much. Her heart is pounding like it's about to explode. The floor continues to rise.

'Enter the code! Now!'

She pushes and a hatch opens immediately in one of the columns. On all fours, Janina hurries towards the exit.

'Slowly, Janina. We don't know what's on the other side.'

But Janina doesn't care about that. She can hear Candela and she hears what she's saying, but she doesn't listen. She needs air. She needs to get out of that hell hole, to run away. Rain or shine, who cares, she just needs to be free, to get out of this nightmare she's trapped in. Right now, she hates Candela; if she could, she would smash the journalist against the wall. She knows that it's not Candela's fault, or at least not all her fault: it's the murderers on the loose, or the damned Orwellians, but Candela got her into this.

Beyond the hatch, a metal ladder rises up above her. Janina doesn't hesitate. She grips the first rung and begins to climb, as fast as she can. Candela tries to persuade her to slow down, but Janina is convinced that there can be nothing worse outside.

'I'm getting out of here!' Janina shouts for Candela to hear over the microphone in the mobile she carries in her pocket.

Her hand grips the last metal rung. Above her, she cannot see the sky. What she does see is a small opening, which she wriggles through. Pulling herself to her feet, she turns and looks behind her. There stands a hexagonal stone table like an altar, with one of its sides missing. That is where she just came out. The room she is in also has six walls, and there is a door in each wall. No signs. Nothing to tell her where they lead to.

'Janina, when you move the camera so fast I can't see anything.'

Janina holds the camera in both hands and slowly turns 360 degrees.

'Tell me which of the six doors I should take, Candela.' Her voice is firm.

'I don't know, I need more information. What's that attached to the ceiling?'

'It looks like a cube, but from this position I can only see three sides. There is a symbol.'

'Go back to the altar you came in through – I didn't get a good look.'

'OK, I'll show you all its sides, then you can tell me the way out of here.'

'Calm down, Janina. I'm going to get you out, but give me time.'

'I'm as calm as I can be, seeing how I am locked in this place. First they tried to cut my hand off, then they nearly crushed me to death. Given the situation, I am very calm, believe me!' she barks.

Tensely, she circles the stone table, finding a new inscription on one side. The text reads:

You have solved the Ministry of Truth. You were not deceived by false appearances and you found the way. Now go to the Ministry of Plenty.

'Stuff that! I'm getting out of here.'

'You can't.'

Janina gives a sarcastic laugh.

'What do you mean, I can't? Who's going to stop me? You? Come here if you think you can.'

66

'Janina, the boss...'

'Leave the boss out of this. He's a better person than you. He wouldn't have put me in here.'

'Yeah, but you can't...'

'I can't what?'

'You can't leave. The first text was clear: *If you want to travel the route, enter the code. But remember, once you start, there is no going back.* Remember? We read it together.'

'But you said...'

'I asked you over and again whether you were sure you wanted to go in. Now there's only one way out and it's by solving the puzzles. We've already beaten one ministry. I'm really proud of you, Janina, you're much braver than you think. Come on, don't give up. Anyway, you have to go on, there's no other choice.'

Candela is speaking the truth. She did ask the girl again and again, but Janina was too proud to listen. Candela is right. Janina is the one who decided to get into this, but she still gets the feeling that, despite everything, the journalist was less than completely straight with her. She never imagined she would have to go through something like this.

'Please send me a detailed photo of the cube on the ceiling.'

'I've sent it. Now I'm going to be sick.'

'Are you alright, Janina?'

The question is purely rhetorical: who could understand Janina's state of mind better than Candela? She wonders how terribly changed the Janina who comes out at the other end of this nightmare journey will be.

She looks closely at the photo from Janina.

'I don't understand it, it looks incomplete and I don't see how it links to everything else. But I'll keep it, I don't think they put it there by chance. It may be useful later. There's a drawing over the altar.'

'I can see it.'

They are back on the road.

TICK-TOCK TICK-TOCK TICK-TOCK TICK-TOCK

SPAM
WEIV TEERTS
51.509617,
-0.082759

You haven't solved the puzzle on this page yet.
Find the code to work out where to continue reading.

If you need to, look at the clues on pages 163–164.

Write the code here so you can remember and refer to it later.

70

YOU HAVE SOLVED THE 1984 PUZZLE

Continued from page 17.

Continued from page 17.

JOHN MILTON'S HOUSE

1,979 minutes

'Taxi!'

Janina gives the taxi driver the address: Berkyn Manor, Stanwell Road, Horton, the house where the writer John Milton lived for a time, according to Candela. Janina has consulted Wikipedia and now she knows that Milton was a famous poet.

The taxi driver made her write down the address for him, as if he couldn't understand it at first. And then he asked her if she was sure she wanted to go there, since strange things linked to the spirit world took place in that house. Janina is not afraid of intangible ghosts and ghouls, she couldn't care less about them. About the other ones, the real ghouls, especially the ones you meet in bars late at night, those she utterly despises. Janina tells the taxi driver to stop talking nonsense and just get her to her destination. And, if possible, to keep quiet on the way. She needs to think.

Janina is uneasy. Candela has given her the chance to get out of this, and in fact, insisted she took it, but there is no way she will accept the journalist's offer. She would do anything for the boss, she loves him so much, more than if he were her real dad. He's the only one who always had faith in her.

She's uneasy and doesn't know if she will measure up to the job she's been given, partly because she doesn't know exactly what she's supposed to do. She didn't want to admit it to Candela, but she knows nothing about anything, about the Orwellians, about Goldstein, about the ministries...

During the journey, she tried to read the copy of *1984* that Candela gave her, but she couldn't concentrate, her mind was in

72

a thousand places at once. She likes people who tell it like it is, but Candela isn't one of those kind of people, at least not with her. All Candela says is that if Janina wants out, that's fine, but she won't tell her exactly what she's going to come up against.

Was flying to London a good idea? It's always the same with her. When someone proposes something, she doesn't know what questions to ask and the doubts only come to mind later. It's the same when she has an argument with someone: it's only much later, once she gets home, that she comes up with the killer line that would settle things once and for all.

And now she doesn't understand the half of it. When Candela told her that they needed to infiltrate that sect or whatever it is (it's true that Candela didn't actually say the word 'sect') and that to do so they would have to pass a series of tests, she didn't really quite understand what the journalist was talking about. And Candela's strange, anyway. What with that ungainly limp and how po-faced she always is, she's a bit scary. But the boss always says he had the most fun ever going out on the town with her before the 'incident', as they all call it. Janina can't imagine Candela being much of a laugh.

But what was she supposed to do? The boss was fighting for his life and Candela said that it was no accident, that they'd tried to kill him. It was hard not to break down in tears and start screaming. How could she not choose to help? How could she have said no? Poor Candela can barely walk! And here she is now, in London, with a backpack like a survival kit, in trouble again. That just about sums her up.

When Janina told the taxi driver she preferred not to talk, he turned on the radio. The news was on.

[...] MP forced to resign after the co-ordinated attack launched by the Orwellians on computers in several banks located in tax havens. The personal details of account holders have been leaked and [...]

73

Janina asks the taxi driver if he knows who the Orwellians are. The driver looks into the rear-view mirror, surprised.

'Everyone in London knows who they are: a bunch of ballsy guys who know what's what,' he replies.

Candela sends Janina a message asking whether she has read the book.

'A bit,' she lies.

'Find out about the Ministry of Truth, that's the first ministry we need to enter, and call me when you get to Milton's house,' Candela commands.

According to the summary she downloaded from the Internet, Orwell wrote the book in the late 1940s. He created a world ruled by Big Brother – who sees everything – in which everything is forbidden: thought, love, desire... Everything. Screens are constantly filming, listening in on what everyone says, even reading their lips if necessary. No one escapes. Individual freedom is quashed.

The Ministry of Truth rewrites history as it pleases. If anything happens that contradicts the past, its workers change the history books. *Just like now with all that about post-truth, strategic communication and all that. This Orwell guy was a visionary,*' thinks Janina.

The boss has blind faith in Candela. He always says she is the smartest woman he ever met, which is why he made Janina enrol for the university course taught by Candela. And he defends her openly when her colleagues at the newspaper say she's become paranoid since the 'incident'. But is getting into all this really the sensible thing to do?

Janina feels guilty for doubting. If the boss believes in Candela, she should too. If the boss respects her, she should too. But she can't help thinking that Candela is a bit of a pain at times.

'I'm there, Candela. What do you want me to do?'

The journey took just 45 minutes. The taxi driver left her outside a house that must have been stately once, but is now in

74

ruins. It's cold, and, although it's almost eleven o'clock in the morning, there is hardly any light.

'Right, Janina, you are my eyes now. Film everything you can on the camera so that I can see what you see. I want you to show me every stone in the damn place. Start by pointing the camera upwards and bringing it down slowly. Then move it a little to one side and up and down again, as if you were painting a door.'

Janina follows Candela's instructions, imagining she is caressing the skin of a guy she likes, but not thinking of anyone in particular; she doesn't want to get distracted.

'There! Keep still! Focus a little further up, Janina.'

'No need to shout, Candela, I can hear you perfectly.'

'The third window on the right, the one that opens by pushing up. Can you see the symbol?'

Janina sees the symbol of the inverted grapes that identifies the Orwellians.

TICK-TOCK TICK-TOCK TICK-TOCK TICK-TOCK

You haven't solved the puzzle on this page yet.
Find the code to work out where to continue reading.

If you need to, you can use the clues on page 164.

Write the code here so you can remember and refer to it later.

YOU HAVE SOLVED THE PUZZLE OF THE MAP

Continued from page 9.

Continued from page 9.

Approximately 34,900,000 results (0.73 seconds).

Candela has begun her fact-hunt where all searches begin: with the obvious. Browser, keyword: *Orwellians*. And there are literally millions of results: news, comments, videos, images, but nothing that tells her where to find them.

Pause, breathe, and start again. She knows that research is method, method and more method, plus a bit of luck.

If she finds nothing where they say you can find anything, then maybe she can find something where everything really *is*. Ninety-six per cent of Internet content is beyond the reach of conventional search engines. So Candela enters the next stage. Using the Tor browser, she enters the Deep Web, the Internet's invisible underworld, which heaves with all kinds of content, both legal and illegal: weapons sales, child pornography, drugs, ads for hackers, for killers... An Internet connected to the very underbelly of society.

You don't search on the Deep Web the same way as you do on the Surface Web. Here, everything is anonymous, clandestine. You can only find what you're looking for if you know where to look, if you have the addresses to get there. Fortunately, Candela Fuertes knows how to find them. Candela is a reporter and, until recently, a leading light in investigative journalism. With a cup of coffee in one hand and computer mouse in the other, she focuses her attention on the screen.

One address leads to another, and that address to one more, and so on, until you lose all track. Start again. One by one, she studies the entries she finds: people who claim to have talked with the leaders of the Orwellians; lists of celebrities of all kinds who, rumour has it, belong to the group; photos of alleged attacks perpetrated by the Orwellians. Maybe some of this information is true, but most is just a smokescreen designed to deceive. Her intuition, which has not abandoned her even for a moment, tells her this, and her experience agrees.

Another dead link. Start again.

The Orwellians are a thorn in the side of the morally questionable powers-that-be. They are experts at hanging out dirty laundry: corruption, money laundering, paedophilia. And they are totally unscrupulous about how they get their information. Nobody knows for sure who is behind the masks, and their anonymity makes them even more dangerous. Are they a group of idealistic madmen and women? No. Doing what they do requires resources and organisation. Also, as their actions are not always – indeed, almost never – legal, it is quite understandable that it should be so hard to reach them.

Another address. A new path to explore.

On her third cup of coffee, Candela finds a site that talks about The Path of Truth. This path would seem to be a kind of rite of passage that anyone seeking to reach the Orwellians must follow, according to the author of the entry. A light bulb goes on inside Candela's head.

She has found a thread to tease out. She just hopes it doesn't break along the way.

Isn't easy, and she loses her way more than once, not unusual in itself. When you enter the Deep Web, things change at the speed of light and where once there was something, now there is nothing. Nevertheless, patiently and methodologically, Candela picks up the thread once more.

She is tired, but he is not going to stop yet, much less now, when it seems that her search is beginning to give fruit. From a phrase to a name, from a name to a list, from a list to a place, from a place to an engraving. Only someone with an exceptional mind could interpret what lies behind that image. And she is just that person. She stares closely at the image and, slowly, things begin to make sense.

Is that the entrance? She needs to reach them as soon as possible. A suspicion has entered her mind.

TICK-TOCK TICK-TOCK TICK-TOCK TICK-TOCK

You haven't solved the puzzle on this page yet.
Find the code to work out where to continue reading.

If you need to, you can use the clues on page 164.

Write the code here so you can remember and refer to it later.

83

YOU HAVE SOLVED THE PUZZLE OF JOHN MILTON'S HOUSE

Continued from page 77.

THE LIBRARY

Janina is entering the house and Candela's heart is in her mouth. She has no idea how Janina will respond to the challenge. *'Too young... it should be me,'* she thinks.

'Put the latex gloves on, they'll help you retain your sense of touch,' she instructs Janina. 'And always look before you take the next step. Careful with the window... Watch out!'

She has to restrain herself from giving orders constantly. She needs to watch now, see how things play out, see how Janina reacts to the tests. So far, she has done everything well. She moves like a cat.

Candela watches as Janina opens the doors to the rooms one by one, showing her what is inside. Dust and objects from the past: old abandoned prams, beds made up ready for guests, a piano with the lid open, some of its keys missing. Until she finds the library, where everything is in total chaos, with books everywhere, some gathering dust on the shelves, others torn and damaged. There are books on the floor, on the armchair...

Candela is not quite sure what to look for, but in the absence of other clues uses her logic. If she had designed the test, this is what she would have done.

'Look for a copy of *1984*,' says Candela. 'I'm not sure, but it may have an eye on the cover.'

'I'm looking, but it's like trying to find a needle in a haystack.'

'If you point the camera, I'll try to help you from here.'

Hoping to see something that will show them the way, Candela concentrates on what Janina is showing her on the camera.

85

Candela knows that it was mostly thanks to instinct that she got out of the maze. *'Janina's inexperienced,'* she thinks. But there's no choice, so better go for it.

Today's paper, which she bought at the hospital newsstand, reminds her why she needs to find the Orwellians.

THE ORWELLIANS STRIKE AGAIN

Hundreds of photographs have been installed around the home of businessman Valerio Martín, showing him meeting different shady characters. It will be difficult for him to explain what he was doing in a restaurant with Vladimir Potska, a leading arms smuggler in [...]

Stories like this appear in the newspapers every day. There can be no doubt that the Orwellians are achieving more results via their unorthodox methods than she is managing to with all her reports and insistent fact-checking.

When the dirt on the Wanstein Club started emerging, a seek-and-destroy mission was launched against her, not just as a journalist, but as a person. Debunkers, those unscrupulous professionals of disinformation – false journalists who write the news without caring if it's true or not and with the sole objective of confusing people and swaying public opinion in a direction that is favourable to their clients – were quick to spring into action.

They went straight for the jugular – there were lots of people thirsty for the blood of 'the most famous investigative journalist of the moment'. *'What a joke!'* thinks Candela. In the collective imagination she soon became labelled as paranoid, obsessed by the smart gentlemen of the Wanstein Club. They won and she lost.

But she is determined to see this through to the bitter end and unmask Castian Warnes, whatever happens.

'Janina, can you see whether the books are classified in any way on the shelves?'

'I don't know whether there is any method, but *1984* isn't here.'

86

She will never know what would have happened if she had kept her mouth shut after escaping from the Daedalus, but that was never her way. They constructed a lie, 'post-truth' as they call it now, and people swallowed their story hook, line and sinker.

'Well, if it's not on the shelves and I'm not wrong, that's the book we're looking for…'

'What?'

'I'm just thinking aloud…'

The boss was always on her side, even when everyone was telling him to sack her, that she was a burden on the paper. Sitting at the end of his bed, Candela gazed at him. Only she and Janina had been to see him. No one else – the boss has no one else.

'Look on the desk nearest to the armchair. In case anyone has been reading it.'

The police had told Janina that the boss's car had sailed over the central reservation on the motorway. For no apparent reason.

'It happens a lot,' they said.

'Well, if it's not on the desk, look on the windowsill. Remember that although it might seem slower, we have to look methodically, combing the whole area.'

Candela's heart had skipped a beat when she entered the hospital room. The boss's forehead was bandaged and gone was all trace of the long hair that had been his style since he was a hippie in the sixties. Nor was he wearing the skull ring that still identified him as a biker, even though it was more than fifteen years since he had last been on a motorbike.

'Look under the furniture in case it fell on the floor,' she tells Janina.

She had never seen him in such a state. His feet, only his forearms brown, his nails stained yellow by nicotine, his eyes rolling uncontrollably in his head, his ears looking so much bigger without his hair…

87

'Candela, what if it's not in the library? What if the person reading it had taken it somewhere else? I read in bed, or…'

'I'm sure it has to be there, Janina. Let me think… Come on, come on…'

The boss was always an excellent driver. It could not have been an accident. And if anyone wanted to kill him, it could only be them, yes, them: the members of the Wanstein Club.

They destroyed her career, but she refused to give up. They slandered her past, but she continued to uncover cases of corruption. They destroyed her health, but she still found the energy to keep on telling the world what she knew. Now they were going for the only thing she could not bear them to harm: the people she loves. And that, Candela Fuertes would never allow, even if it cost her whatever life she had left.

'Janina, have you found anything yet?'

TICK-TOCK TICK-TOCK TICK-TOCK TICK-TOCK

You haven't solved the puzzle on this page yet.
Find the code to work out where to continue reading.

If you need to, you can use the clues on page 164.

Write the code here so you can remember and refer to it later.

YOU HAVE SOLVED THE PUZZLE OF THE FIRST NEXUS

Continued from page 70.

A LONG ROAD

1.855 minutes

The Orwellians have claimed responsibility for the action that led to the resignation of the US ambassador in Paris. This morning, the Embassy was surrounded by photos of the ambassador engaged in sexual activities.

Before starting out on the path as instructed by Candela, Janina eats a couple of energy bars and sips some water. According to the solution they found to the puzzle of the altar, their next destination is a place called St Dunstan in the east. According to Candela's calculations, it is about seven hours away, assuming that the tunnels are more or less straight. She started out just over two hours ago. Candela thought that they were on the right track, but she had not expected such long distances. Yet another challenge. They have to take time and endurance into account. She hopes that Janina is physically fit enough.

St Dunstan was once a church, but the building was badly damaged during the German bombing of London in World War II. All that remains standing now are part of the walls and one of the towers. Today, the site is a public garden where Londoners come to escape from the City for a bit of peace and quiet.

'It must be lovely to sit on one of those benches to wait for a pigeon to shit on your head. Shame I have to travel underground like a rat.'

The last thing she fancies is a seven-hour hike through these tunnels.

'What's that, Janina?'

'Nothing, Candela, I'm talking to myself. By the way, please

92

do me a favour. Tell me everything you need to tell me now, then leave me alone as I walk.'

'I can't leave you alone down there.'

'I don't mean literaly leave me alone. I'll keep the mobile phone on and I'll call you if necessary, but I need to think. Candela, I need you out of my life for a few hours. Understand?'

Of course she understands. More than Janina imagines. She knows that the girl needs to wind down after all the adrenaline that has been coursing through her for the last few minutes. She needs time to digest everything that is going on, to calm down a little.

Candela gives in to Janina's request. She does not like the idea, but agrees and sends a WhatsApp of the map of tunnels she downloaded, asking Janina to keep the locator on her mobile phone activated. That way, she will know where Janina is at all times and will be able to guide her if she thinks her young colleague is getting lost.

'I marked the point you have to reach in red. That's where we should find the Ministry of Plenty. According to *1984*, this was the ministry concerned with feeding the "proles", as they called them. But they only gave them just enough food to stop them dying, while always keeping them on the brink of starvation. And to add insult to injury, they sometimes reduced their rations: instead of three ounces of chocolate, they gave them two. And then they sold it as great achievement, as if they were actually giving them more. And the people swallowed it because, if not, they would wind up with nothing. Another form of control.'

'So, they kept these proles hungry, but didn't kill them, right? And didn't they riot when their rations were reduced and the government played them for fools?'

'No, because most people believed what they were told. It's not so different from what's happening today. A politician comes along and promises whatever, then they don't deliver, but it doesn't matter. People continue to vote for the same corrupt politicians

93

who rob them every day. Lots of moaning and complaining, but in the end we believe any story they throw at us, don't we? Well, it's the same in *1984.*'

'OK, but why St Dunstan? Why a church?'

'I don't know, maybe because when God shuts a door He always opens a window?'

Candela wanted to make Janina smile, but doubts she succeeded.

'Well, I'll leave the mobile on, so if you need anything just call, OK?'

'OK.

'Godspeed.'

'Candela… If something happens to the boss, you'll let me know, won't you?'

'Of course I will, but for now they tell me his situation is stable.'

Janina sets out on her long journey.

1,850 minutes

Janina hangs up. Candela is alone with the boss in the hospital room. There is no time to lose, anything and everything she can find out now may be vital for Janina later. So she checks the map she downloaded. It shows a lot of abandoned underground tunnels. A kind of subterranean dead city. No wonder they used all this infrastructure to install a kind of initiatory journey to hell. Candela looks at her mobile phone screen. The red dot that is Janina is moving pretty fast. *'Good girl!'*

Not so long ago she herself was young, she had that energy, that courage. Some might say just yesterday, but for her a lifetime has passed. Many would say that she is still young but no, that's no longer true. She ceased being young when she got out of the Daedalus. The Candela that everyone knew was left behind. She wonders what Janina will be like when she gets out of all this. *'Because she's going to get out,'* she promises. Candela could never forgive herself otherwise.

When she was looking for information about the Orwellians in the Deep Web, she found some images that she did not show Janina. Images she should have deleted, but which she keeps to remind herself of what they are up against. She looks at them once more. Mutilated bodies fill the screen with horror. They are some of those who tried to travel to the end of the Path of Truth but did not make it. But that does not scare her. *'None of that is going to happen to Janina,'* she mutters. She will make sure of that. Janina is merely the person taking the path that she can no longer follow, in order to reach the end.

95

What frightens her is how cold she felt when she examined those images for the first time, how coolly she had thought up her plan and the lack of feeling that had enabled her to persuade Janina to enter the very jaws of danger. That is what really scares her: the fact that she has changed, that she is no longer herself.

If the Wanstein Club gets away with it and the boss dies, the last person who knew her well enough to remember that she was once good will have been swept off the face of the earth.

Her head aches. She should use these dead hours to sleep a little, but she knows she can't, not until all this is over. There will be time to rest, afterwards.

So she closes the horrifying images and starts checking through all the information and reviews – everything she knows about Orwell – the ministries, the maps...

There is just one thought in her head, one goal.

Revenge.

1,428 MINUTES

Janina has been walking for hours. Cramp-inducing tiredness has at least calmed her a little and rid her of her rage and desire to punch Candela.

She has accepted that she cannot get out, that she needs to act smart if she is to survive. She has even managed to relax a little and overcome her fear. Her friends used to laugh when she said she could let her mind go blank. Of course, they knew nothing of the violent moods that affected her as a child.

From time to time a noise made her jump, but this place is full of noises and she eventually got used to it. There must be a London Underground line nearby, as she occasionally hears the distant sound of what seems to be trains, rattling along the rails. There is also the noise of running water, probably from the sewers. There's a nasty smell. And from time to time, she hears what sound like screams. That's the worst part. She has persuaded herself that it must be some animal. If anyone wanted to kill her, they would have done it by now, but even if it is an animal, it's not much consolation. And she always has the feeling that someone is watching her. *'Relax, Janina.'*

Although she would like to tell the journalist to go to hell, she knows she has to work with Candela, because, as things stand, that represents her only chance of emerging victorious from this mess she has got into up to her neck. The problem is, she is not sure whether Candela knows what she is up against. Because if there is one thing Janina is certain of, it is that these guys are raving mad. She was surrounded by mad people when she was on the street. Heck, she was mad herself. That is why she can smell them a mile off. They are usually people who don't care whether they live or die themselves, let alone whether anybody else lives or dies. And there's something about Candela… No, not Candela, Janina is sure the journalist would never hurt her. Candela loves her people, and the boss is one of her people. And she, Janina, is one of the boss's people.

Candela is awake. Janina is aware of this because whenever she loses her way and takes the wrong tunnel, the journalist is there to put her back on the right track. Though there is really no need. Every time she goes the wrong way, it turns out to be a dead end sooner or later. She is locked in.

And so on she goes, putting one foot in front of the other, all the while trying to make believe she is somewhere else. What she wouldn't give for a nice shower! She hasn't even got any clean underwear she can change into. It wasn't on Candela's list. It's more than a person should have to bear.

The phone rings.

'Hello, Candela.'

'How's it going? Are you very tired? Stupid question, I guess.'

'Whatever… How's the boss?'

'Still with us.'

'…'

'According to the map, you're about to arrive. Keep your eyes peeled. Have you seen anything so far?'

98

'Yes, something really weird. A screwdriver with letters on the handle. I'm sending you a photo of it.'

Two minutes later, Janina sees something shining brightly in the distance. She points the camera so that Candela sees it too. Then they hear the most terrifying sound. The noise is coming from behind and is getting louder and louder. Neither of them knows what it is, but Candela screams 'Run!' down the phone.

'Run towards the light!'

'There's a door, I zoomed in on the picture and can see it. Get there as quick as you can, I don't like that noise at all.'

'The ground is shaking! Something's coming! What is it, Candela?'

'Run! There's no time to waste!'

Candela was right, there is a door at the end of the tunnel. Janina gets there at last, determined to push it open with all her might, kick it open if necessary. Unfortunately, though, as expected, it is locked. The noise is unbearably loud. She spins around, but can't believe her eyes. A wall is rushing towards her at uncanny speed. It's like the scene in *Raiders of the Lost Ark* when the giant boulder is chasing Indiana Jones around the temple. Only, instead of a boulder, it's a wall. And it's going to crush her to death. No, more than a wall, it looks like an open box with the bottom missing. She covers her head. But then, just one metre from the door, it stops. The sides fit perfectly against the wall, boxing her in completely, trapping her. She breathes a huge sigh of relief. She's closed in, but she's still alive. In front of her is a door with a sign saying *Ministry of Plenty*. And above the sign, what looks like some kind of ivory horn. Now, as if a tap had opened inside it, grains of cereal start to pour from this horn, covering the floor in the tiny space she is trapped in. Trickling out, the grain begins to form a pile at her feet.

'The Horn of Plenty!' Candela exclaims.

'And what's that supposed to mean?'

'It means that if I don't get you out, the grain will build up in there until you suffocate. According to the myth, food flows from the horn continuously, so you need to find something that gives us a clue. How high is the grain now?'

'It's just beginning to cover my feet... Wait, Candela, there's something here!'

She bends over and uses her hands to sweep the floor of the cubicle she is trapped in, but the grain continues to flow in, and she can't show Candela the sketch that has appeared at her feet. So she takes out the silver foil thermal blanket that she carries in her backpack and ties one end to the doorknob. She secures the other end to her backpack and uses one hand to hold the blanket up, making an improvised tent. This gives her the brief respite she needs to use her other hand to brush away the grain on the floor under the blanket and show Candela the sketch.

That's my girl! thinks Candela. And her mood begins to swing upwards once more. *I'm going to solve this puzzle. We'll get you out of here. I promise,* she mutters to herself as she starts to examine the sketch.

TICK-TOCK TICK-TOCK TICK-TOCK TICK-TOCK

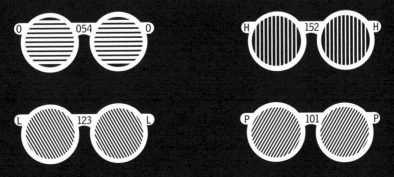

You haven't solved the puzzle on this page yet.
Find the code to work out where to continue reading.

If you need to, you can use the clues on page 164.

Write the code here so you can remember and refer to it later.

102

YOU HAVE SOLVED THE PUZZLE OF THE MINISTRY OF PEACE

Continued from page 63.

316
minutes

Janina turns on the tap and waits. The gauge on the wall shows 1.60, then 2.10, then, 2.70... Then it stops.

Janina is swimming, about 30 centimetres below the sluice gate. She's a good swimmer, she learned as a very young girl. However, she does not know how long she can hold out. She has tried to open the gate, but it is locked. She knows that the answer is in the words written there and which were invisible from below, but she is unable to decode them. She screams with all her might, from anger and from fear, but all it does is make her more tired. She tries to think what Candela would do, but has no idea.

'Think, Janina, think, you have to solve this on your own,' she says, as she treads water to stay afloat.

And then it comes to her: *'The map!'*

TICK-TOCK TICK-TOCK TICK-TOCK TICK-TOCK

104

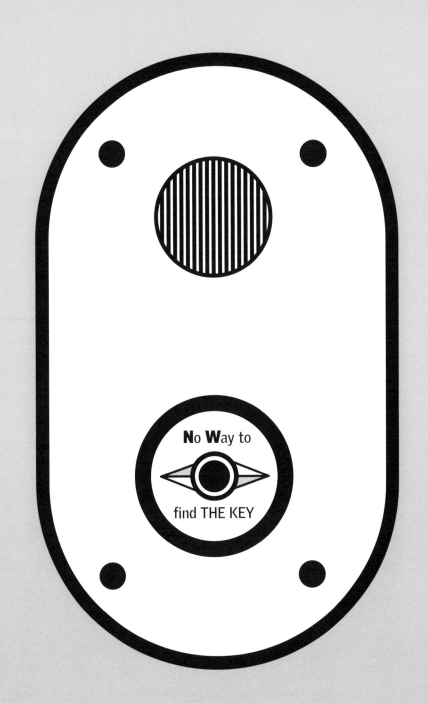

No Way to

find THE KEY

You haven't solved the puzzle on this page yet.
Find the code to work out where to continue reading.

If you need to, you can use the clues on page 165.

Write the code here so you can remember and refer to it later.

106

YOU HAVE SOLVED THE PUZZLE OF ROOM 101

Continued from page 46.

10 minutes

By the time Candela manages to open the door, the rats are clinging to her trainers and trying to bite through them. She swings her feet to get rid of the rats and they all go flying. She closes the door as quickly as she can, leaning against it to get her breath back. When she turns round, what she sees makes her blood run cold.

She is in an interrogation room, just like the ones you see in the movies: a table, chairs, a two-way mirror (one of those mirrors in which they can see you, but you can't see them). The room differs from the interrogation rooms in the movies in one detail only: a glass screen divides the room into two absolutely symmetrical halves. On one side is Candela and on the other is Janina, her hands tied together and rat bites all over her body. Behind the girl, an enormous digital clock shows the minutes and seconds that remain before time is up. Exactly 9.24, 9.23, 9.22… Below is an explosive device connected to the clock.

Candela throws herself against the glass screen and shouts Janina's name. The girl does not even look at her. She stares with glazed eyes at the wall behind Candela.

'Janina, tell me you can hear me! I'm going to get you out, I promise, I'll get you out of here!!!'

Janina does not answer. Only the expression in her eyes changes slightly. She heard her, but she does not want to talk to her.

8.16, 8.15, 8.14…

Candela turns to see what Janina is looking at. A large screen showing some film footage. A motorway. Cars moving towards the camera. *'It's Sabadell.'* Suddenly, one car flies over the central reservation, crashing straight into a lorry. *'Is that the boss's car?'* The sequence is repeated over and over again, on a loop... *'Boss!'* Now, in slow motion, the camera zooms in. The driver of the car comes into view. There is no doubt that it's him. Candela bursts into tears at the sight of his face, his hair, his hands on the steering wheel. He's clearly singing. Then he takes out a cigarette, lights it, then fumbles it from his hand... Instinctively, he tries to catch it... Then, suddenly, his car is flying over the central reservation and... the screen goes black. Then the film starts up again.

Stunned, Candela stares at the screen. She cannot tear her gaze away from those images. She doesn't want to turn around, to face Janina, but she has to. She feels as if she's about to faint and so sits down on the chair. She turns around. Janina is no longer looking at the screen but is staring at her, Candela.

6.40, 6.39, 6.38...

'You lied. It wasn't attempted murder. It was a bloody accident.'

Candela had never felt so humiliated, so disgusting, so full of self-loathing. They had fooled her, yet again. She, and she alone, was responsible for Janina's present state.

She decides not to even attempt to explain to Janina that she had really believed it was not an accident. That she truly believed that members of the Wanstein Club had tried to kill the boss. She decides not to try, because she knows that Janina will not believe her, whatever she says.

4
minutes

But Janina is right. She did lie. She has deceived her all along. Not because of the boss. She really believed that it had been attempted murder. No, that's not it. *'Boss, forgive me.'*

She deceived Janina because she did not tell her that she had always believed that Castian was behind the Orwellians. And, despite everything, she had shown no mercy, but had dragged Janina into this hell.

Not one conviction, not a single member of the club had been exposed to public scorn and disgust. Not a single one! They were so skilful at manipulating people, at diverting people's attention towards other things and then getting rid of their enemies. She had suspected it the day she received the offer of the chance to meet them. They had also invited her to the Daedalus.

She had suspected it the day she saw the terrifying images of those who had tried to reach the Path of Truth before them on the Deep Web. Only a very sick mind could do that. Although, thinking about it, perhaps it was all a set-up to draw her in and finish off the little that remained of Candela Fuertes.

Once again he has her at his mercy and again they will meet eye to eye, face to face. Because Candela is sure that behind that two-way mirror is the man who manipulated her until she revealed her very worst side. A puppet, controlled by a repellent guy whose name she cannot even remember.

'Are you going to leave me here to die? What have you done to me, Candela? What have you done to me? Why?' sobs Janina.

110

Janina's screams bring Candela back to reality. The clock continues its countdown: 3.59, 3.58, 3.57...

By his evil arts, Castian Warnes has turned Candela Fuertes, once a good journalist and an even better person, into the worst piece of shit on the face of the Earth. She realises this. But now is not the time to examine her conscience.

What she has to do now is to get Janina out of there. She owes it to her friend, she owes it to the boss and she owes it to herself.

Candela turns her back on the two-way mirror and looks at Janina. She makes a pleading gesture, asking the girl for forgiveness. She takes a gun from her jacket pocket. It's a small pistol. Wide-eyed, Janina stares at her in terror. *'Does she really believe I'd kill her? This is the monster they have turned me into,'* thinks Candela.

Then, her pistol hidden in her hand, Candela Fuertes turns, looks straight into the mirror and fires.

The mirror shatters, and the first thing she sees are eyes she hasn't seen for a long time. Castian's gaze is filled not with surprise, but with admiration. Candela raises the gun again, aims at his forehead and shoots. Castian Warnes dies. 3.01, 3.00, 2.59... Janina is weeping pitifully on other side of the screen. The clock shows 2.56 until the bomb goes off.

TICK-TOCK TICK-TOCK TICK-TOCK TICK-TOCK

02.56

14 + 25 + 32 + 44 + 73 + 6

You haven't solved the puzzle on this page yet.
Find the code to work out where to continue reading.

If you need to, you can use the clues on page 165.

Write the code here so you can remember and refer to it later.

113

YOU HAVE SOLVED THE PUZZLE OF THE MINISTRY OF PLENTY

Continued from page 159.

1,415 minutes

'Janina, enter the key, for God's sake!'

'Candela…' Her voice is no more than a whisper.

'Janina, please, get your act together!'

'I can't, Candela, I just can't – I haven't got the strength.'

Candela understands all too well what the girl is saying, but even so, her anger rises. She won't let Janina throw in the towel. Not now. She would never forgive herself. *If only I had had a friendly voice to guide me when I entered the Daedalus,* she thinks. She knows that she is being unfair, that her thought is totally unfair.

'Janina, please, don't let us down, not now. He would be so proud of you.'

'He would never have put me in danger, Candela…' Janina replies in a weak voice.

'You don't know that. People change a lot when someone has tried to wipe them out. Believe me, I know what I'm talking about,' she finishes, with a hint of irony.

'Not him.'

Candela knows this is true, that the boss would never have put anyone in danger.

Not him. *She* would, though. Candela is trapped in a vicious circle that will not grind to a halt until she rids the world of Castian Warnes. When she entered the Daedalus, she persuaded herself that she had done it for the good of humanity. In the same tone of voice, she says:

'Well… If you want, we can ask him later.'

115

Today, Candela knows that she was lying to herself. That all she really wants is to wipe out the man who destroyed her.

'Is he awake? Has the boss woken up?' asks Janina, suddenly more lively.

'No, not yet, but the doctors tell me he will soon. You're right, if he wakes up and finds out you're trapped, he'll have a heart attack. You don't want him to come round and find you here, do you? We need to get out as quick as possible.'

And to get out, to destroy Castian Warnes, she will do anything necessary.

'The boss is going to recover!'

She can indulge in some good self-loathing later.

Janine dredges up some strength, pulls herself to her feet and enters the key Candela sent her.

The gas stops entering, the water stops flowing and the cylinder disappears back into the ceiling. In the ground, a staircase appears, leading downwards.

Janina does not even ask Candela. She goes down the steps into a hexagonal room identical to the one at the rear of the Ministry of Truth. Here, too, there is part of a cube on the ceiling, six paths and a hexagonal altar, on which are inscribed some letters. On the wall, a phrase is written. Janina reads it aloud:

> You have solved the Ministry of Plenty. You were not blinded by the fear of breaking with convention, and you found the way out. Now go to the Ministry of Peace.

More than six-hundred miles away, Candela takes note. She lied to Janina: the boss is not getting better. There will be time to ponder all this. Right now, she's hot on the trail of her prey. The hunter inside her is fired up. The journey continues.

TICK-TOCK TICK-TOCK TICK-TOCK TICK-TOCK

116

You haven't solved the puzzle on this page yet.
Find the code to work out where to continue reading.

If you need to, you can use the clues on page 165.

Write the code here so you can remember and refer to it later.

118

YOU HAVE SOLVED THE PUZZLE OF THE LIBRARY

Continued from page 90.

1,905 minutes

Janina points the camera and Candela observes. As if she were there, as if they were together. Candela needs to see every tiny detail, and Janina wants to make sure they miss nothing.

'This house gives me the creeps. It feels as if they're watching me.'

Candela is almost certain that this is the case, but says nothing. She doesn't want Janina to give free reign to her imagination and become her own worst enemy. Better for her not to know for certain; that way, her fear can stay under control and they will make better progress.

Behind the books they removed from the shelves was a copy of *1984*. There is a key between its pages.

'Are you wearing the gloves?'

'Yes.

'Pick it up, carefully.'

She can't take the risk that the key is coated in some kind of poisonous substance.

'What does it smell like?'

Janina holds it close to her nose and sniffs.

'Dunno, like an old key?'

Candela smiles. *'She's so young. I won't let anything happen to her!'*

'Okay, Janina, now we just need to find a lock for that key. We need to try all the locks, so start with the ones on your right and go around until you get back to the library again. Go as fast as you can, time's running out.'

'Candela, I need to pee...'

120

'...'

'I need to pee, I tell you!'

'Well, go on then, pee.'

'I'm turning the camera off, OK?'

'...'

'I'm not going to pee with the camera on, it's weird!'

'Conspiracy? Murder? Do you know what you're saying? Shouldn't we go to the police? This is all a bit much, isn't it?' Janina had exclaimed when Candela informed her that the alleged accident was no accident at all. But Candela had cleverly fed the younger girl just enough information to prevent her from going to the police and instead agree to help her.

Candela knows that the girl is not really up to it, but she's smart. Six-hundred miles away, Janina will act as her body double. Candela also knows that Janina is rather in awe of her, which stopped her from asking too many questions. Candela took advantage of the situation, but is determined not to let anything happen to her young colleague. It is all for a just cause. The Wanstein Club has gone too far.

'Everything alright? Can we get on now?' asks Candela.

'Yes.'

Janina follows Candela's orders to the letter. Step by step. Concentrating hard.

'Good.'

Sensibly, methodically.

'Good.'

Candela starts to relax a little. Perhaps they have a chance after all. She looks at her watch and sees that over an hour has gone by since they started. *The secret is to keep going, slowly but surely,*' thinks Candela.

The Orwellians could not have chosen a better time or a better name for themselves. This is the first time we have had access to so much information. Most people think that this brings transparency, but the information that reaches the public is only a tiny part of the whole; only what they want us to have. Big Data is our own Big Brother. Technology controls us, but we love it because it tells us where our loved ones are. It rules us and makes us dependent on it and, when it breaks down, we feel like abandoned children, lost in the centre of the big city. We join all the social networks in order to connect with people when, at heart, we have never been so alone. The Internet of Things. The world's new Big Brother.

'Candela, I'm back at the library door. No luck. The key didn't open anything.'

'We're missing something... Look on the library floor!'

'...'

'Alright, then. Show me everything on the camera again, slowly, please.'

'Candela, there's a book by John Milton here...'

Janina bends down to pick it up, but the book is firmly fixed to the floor. She blows the dust off it and uses her fingers to clean the floor around it. Then she opens the book cover and sees a lock.

'Well done, Janina, you found it! Put the key in, I'm certain we've reached the Ministry of Truth.'

'But this is like the lock on a safe...'

'But there's a tumbler lock you can put the key in. Do you see it? Try that!'

'It doesn't work.'

'But I'm sure that's the entrance. We just need to find out how to open the trapdoor.'

TICK-TOCK TICK-TOCK TICK-TOCK TICK-TOCK

122

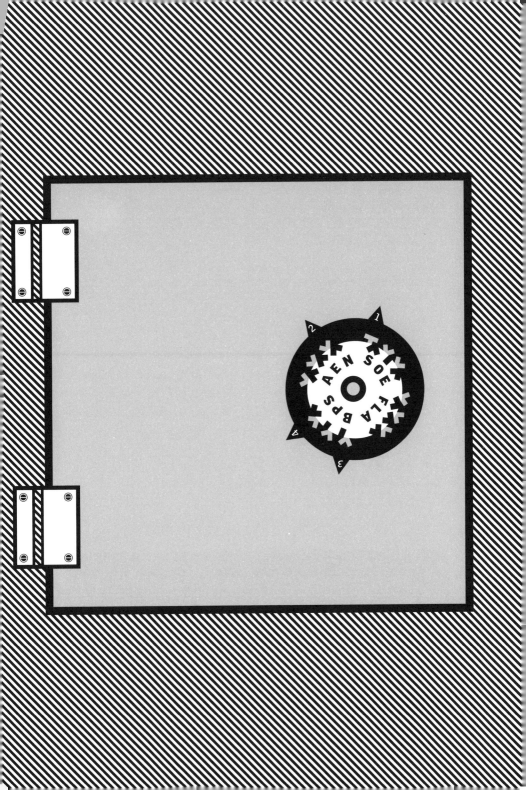

You haven't solved the puzzle on this page yet.
Find the code to work out where to continue reading.

If you need to, you can use the clues on page 165.

Write the code here so you can remember and refer to it later.

YOU HAVE SOLVED THE PUZZLE OF THE MINISTRY OF LOVE

Continued from page 57.

THE GRAVESTONE

'Janina, Janina, Janina, Janina...' whispers Candela.

With every second that passes without news from Janina, her body doubles up more. She can hardly bear the pain in her stomach. She knows that the girl got into the coffin, that the lid closed and that she screamed her head off calling for help. Whoever dreamed up this nightmare wanted Janina to feel completely alone, and for Candela to feel she had abandoned her to her fate.

Afterwards, a graveyard silence. She can't understand how her mobile has gone offline. Someone must have cut it off.

She has to get to Janina, she has to get in, come what may. The red dot has disappeared. She has lost all connection with the girl. Candela bends down and starts scratching at the earth with her bare hands. She thinks she hears voices, then realises what she is doing. If anyone sees they will think she has gone mad, and they would be right. That is what they want, what this is all about: to drive her crazy and then point it out for the world to see.

'You see? Candela Fuertes is crazy, she always has been.'

Suddenly, she comes face to face with a gravestone on which someone has painted the name GOLDSTEIN, the leader of the revolution in *1984*. The paint is still wet. There can be no doubt. They painted it for her to see. She pushes the stone but, as anticipated, it doesn't even move. Then she sees some lines and an idea comes to her. Candela gets down to work.

'I'm coming, Janina, hang on just a bit longer!'

126

TICK-TOCK TICK-TOCK TICK-TOCK TICK-TOCK

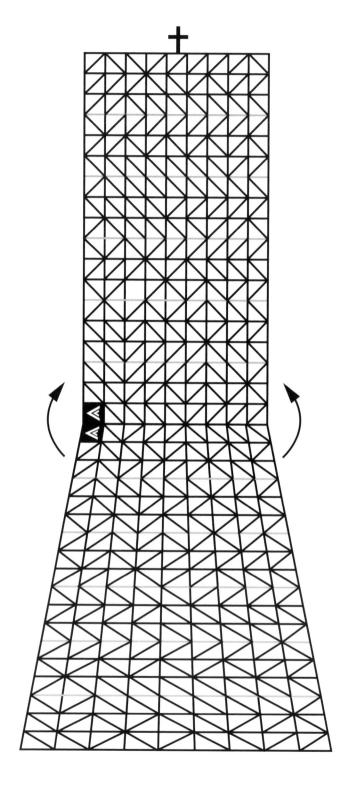

You haven't solved the puzzle on this page yet.
Find the code to work out where to continue reading.

If you need to, you can use the clues on page 165–166.

Write the code here so you can remember and refer to it later.

YOU HAVE SOLVED THE PUZZLE OF THE PATH OF TRUTH

Continued from page 83.

At last, she has found the entrance to the Path of Truth or, at least, a website with minimal credibility that tells you how to do so. Candela reads carefully:

> We, the Orwellians, are the true guardians, the only ones that can stop the establishment.

'That's just bluff and bluster,' she mutters to herself. Maybe she got it wrong and they are just a band of loonies with delusions of grandeur after all.

She has always had mixed feelings about them, but recently she had begun to take them more seriously. *'Maybe I'm making a mistake,'* she thinks. The Orwellians really do uncover scandals, shining the spotlight on corrupt politicians, bankers and military big cheeses. They have plenty of means at their disposal and use extraordinary stunts to make their stories known to the public. They are real artists at getting their information across to people.

The Orwellians know that most people only read the sports section when leafing through the newspaper, and that many change channel as soon as the news comes on. Their view is that merely informing is not enough, that information can be manipulated, that it is necessary to go much further to make the truth heard, which is why they organise the most amazing publicity stunts: dressing up a cathedral as a bride, throwing red paint all over the European Parliament and so on. And what's more, they have yet to be caught.

Even so, Candela still has her doubts. *'Do I really need to try to find them?'*

The problem is that they sometimes get it wrong and shine their spotlight on those who are innocent. And when that happens, the damage they cause is irreparable. Doubts about the person in question take a long time to dissipate, and, as she sees it, the Orwellians get it wrong far too often. She remembers reading a comment claiming that it was worth the risk, as ninety per cent of the time the Orwellians got it right. *'What about the other ten per cent? Who cares?'* No, Candela finds that kind of scattergun approach unacceptable.

According to the Orwellians, we are living under the yoke of Big Brother, who surveils, manipulates and controls us all. We may not believe it, but we have lost the capacity to think for ourselves. All that information has intoxicated us. The powers-that-be bombard us with the news they want us to hear to distract us from what is really happening. 'The invisible threat', they call it. We live in a world like the one Orwell imagined in his novel *1984*, hence the name of the group.

Basically speaking, Candela agrees with them. Some time ago she literally risked her life by entering the Daedalus, the macabre security system invented by the finance magnate Castian Warnes. She managed to unmask the members of the Wanstein Club, powerful people who wanted to destroy the euro and sink the European economy. Candela had thwarted them and yet she had lost. Yes, she took them to court, but they were all soon safely back at home again. She continued to attack them and they continued to hound her. Whenever she published some new case of dirty tricks by club members, the papers were flooded with stories that tarnished her reputation and questioned her integrity. They gradually undermined her authority. She fought back, but they finally destroyed her career as a journalist and almost finished her off as a person, too.

132

She risked her life, but no judge would sentence them as their crimes merited. Something inside her had died as she slowly realised that sometimes, the truth counts for nothing. *'Dammit, I deserved better.'*

And yet, up to now, Candela has held on firmly to her principles, red lines that she has never crossed. That is why she just filed the Orwellians' invitation away.

But what has happened now changes everything. She is going to reach the Orwellians. In their quest for truth, they have achieved much more by performing their crazy stunts than she has with all her bleeding-heart, honest-to-god truths, and she will stop the Wanstein Club in its tracks.

Sitting at her desk, Candela puts her coffee down. She concentrates hard. She must reach the Path of Truth.

We, the Orwellians, ask: Why does no one stand up against the brutal wave of oppression and criminal activity that is affecting society?

Day after day there are fresh revelations about cases of corruption, child abuse, theft, gender violence, deaths of immigrants, evictions, former politicians becoming rich at the expense of their fellow citizens, major brands exploiting children...

Why doesn't a revolution break out to wake up a world in which everyone seems to have fallen asleep? How is it possible that even equipped with all this information, we do not overthrow our rulers?

The answer is simple: THE TRUTH NO LONGER MATTERS.

'That's exactly right, guys. Are you talking to me?' Candela is almost certain she has found the way in. She still has her doubts; they are probably just a bunch of crazies and she is just wasting her time, but she hasn't got much to lose. She has fought with all her might to bring down the Wanstein Club while sticking to the rules, and got precisely nowhere. It's time to take a new approach.

THE FIRST STEP

'Hello, Janina.'

Janina had given Candela the news that had driven the journalist over the edge. The news that had forced her to take the decision to go all out, whatever happened, whatever the cost.

First, disbelief: when she read the WhatsApp message she was certain there must be some mistake.

> Hello, Candela. It's Janina. I've got some bad news for you. The boss's car went over the central reservation on the motorway and crashed straight into a lorry going the other way. He is in a critical state in the intensive care unit at City Hospital. The doctors say his life is in danger. I'm sorry I couldn't find a gentler way to tell you this.

Second, distress. The boss has had a car accident and is fighting for his life. So strong until a few hours ago, now so weak.

Third, impotence. It can't have been an accident. Something tells Candela that someone has tried to kill the boss, the most important person in her life right now.

Fourth, revenge. Only someone looking to hurt *her* could try to kill the boss. She doesn't need any more details to know who the murderer is. Nothing can stop her going after them with everything she's got.

They are sitting beside the bed where the boss lies on life support.

Janina is the new intern on the paper, the boss's god-daughter. She is twenty-one and, until recently, the boss had never even mentioned this young girl that he treats like the daughter he never had, at least to Candela. She never asked, and he never told. That is the nature of their relationship. They don't need to know everything to love and admire each other.

'Did you find it?' asks Janina.

'I think so.'

Candela shows her the screen on her laptop and they read the message on the Orwellians' website. Candela likes Janina. If only she had had a choice and could have avoided asking the girl to do this. However, the weakness caused by the chronic illness she has had since she breathed in the poisonous gas in the Daedalus has forced her to find someone to undertake the journey she is physically unable to make herself.

Many claim to be good people but in reality they hide their heads in the sand. Only those who are willing to follow the Path of Truth are worthy of becoming Orwellians. You do not know who we are, but we know who you are. If you want to take the path, enter the code. But remember, once you start, there is no going back.

You will have 1,984 minutes to reach Goldstein. If you are unsuccessful, it will be all over for you.

ENTER KEY

The two hesitate, each looking at the other.

'It says enter key.'

'I know.'

'What key?'

'No idea!'

'And who is Goldstein?'

'The supposed leader of the rebellion in the novel *1984*.

'Ah.'

Candela can see that Janina has no idea who this Goldstein is, but what does that matter? She is so young! Her short hair is cut unevenly but not because it is the fashion. No, Candela would swear she cuts it herself. She wears jeans two sizes too big for her, and hand-painted cotton T-shirts. They don't know each other well, but Candela is convinced that her only chance is to set out on this journey with Janina. That or nothing.

The two women, one a journalist who looks older than her years and the other a student who looks younger than the age on her passport, gaze at the Orwellians' website, trying to find the key. At times, life throws odd couples together.

TICK-TOCK TICK-TOCK TICK-TOCK TICK-TOCK

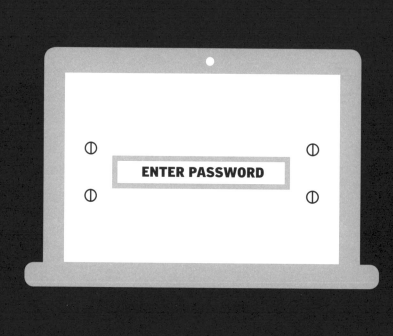

ENTER PASSWORD

You haven't solved the puzzle on this page yet.
Find the code to work out where to continue reading.

If you need to, you can use the clues on page 166.

Write the code here so you can remember and refer to it later.

YOU HAVE SOLVED THE PUZZLE OF THE TRAPDOOR

Continued from page 106.

She did it by herself. The trapdoor is open. Janina kicks her legs and pushes up so that she can hang on to the edges of the opening to rest a little before continuing. She is not strong enough to pull herself up, not yet.

The walls go up and up as far as she can see and she can't see where they end. It looks like a narrower continuation of the cistern. There is a ladder. She'll have to push herself high out of the water in order to grab it, so she takes a deep breath and heaves herself towards the first rung.

TICK-TOCK TICK-TOCK TICK-TOCK TICK-TOCK

In the hospital, Candela is still waiting for Janina's call. She dials the girl's number. No reply.

Sitting on the boss's bed, looking down at him, she starts to cry. 'I'm sorry, I'm sorry, I'm sorry,' she repeats over and over. She knows she is a murderer, that if Janina dies, it will be her fault and no one else's, but she would do it again. Anything to reach them.

'I'm going to kill you, Castian Warnes. I'm going to kill you.'

She says it out loud, as if someone could hear her. She knows that someone can.

Candela is getting ready to leave when her phone rings.

'Janina! Thank God! How are you? *Where* are you?'

'Sitting in the middle of a hexagonal room like the other ones, dripping wet.'

141

For the first time since they first met, Janina hears Candela laugh. Surprisingly, her laughter has a pleasant ring to it that gives a glimpse of the woman she once was.

'How much time have we got left?'

'About five hours.'

'Then there's no time to waste. This room is the same as the others. I'll send you a picture of the cube in this one, just in case. There is also a text:

You have solved the Ministry of Peace. You found help in the unknown, and found balance. Now go to the Ministry of Love.

Candela's blood runs cold, and she struggles not to betray her feelings as she speaks to Janina.

'Janina, are there any symbols on the altar?'

'Yes, some crosses. Sending photos now.'

Candela knows what awaits them at the Ministry of Love.

TICK-TOCK TICK-TOCK TICK-TOCK TICK-TOCK

142

You haven't solved the puzzle on this page yet.
Find the code to work out where to continue reading.

If you need to, you can use the clues on page 166.

Write the code here so you can remember and refer to it later.

144

YOU HAVE SOLVED THE PUZZLE
OF THE DOOR OF TRUTH

Continued from page 25.

It worked. Janina pulls out her hand. Euphoric, Candela feels the adrenaline rushing through her veins.

'Boss, my brain is still in good shape,' she says, as if he could hear her.

Tears are streaming down Janina's face. Who cares whether or not Candela hears her crying! She massages her bruised wrist. She knows that the door is open because she heard a click, but she has not yet tried it. She needs a minute to pull herself together. She should never have agreed, she should never have let herself be persuaded by Candela for a number of reasons, among them the fact that she is sure the boss would never have approved of what the journalist is doing. He would never have placed her in danger. How could she have been so naïve!

And she is right. Candela is convinced that, if the boss woke up and found out that she had sent Janina on the trail of the Orwellians, he would never forgive her. All she can hope is that her instinct doesn't let her down and everything goes as planned. *'All in good time,'* she reassures herself. Now is not the time to hesitate – there can be no turning back. She has to keep moving towards her final goal, that of bringing down the Wanstein Club.

'The door's open. You need to go in, Janina.'

'Candela, do you really think we can trust the Orwellians? Because to me they seem more like a bunch of psychopaths than anything else.'

'You're right, Janina. Their way of recruiting members is unconventional, I agree, but they're not conventional themselves.

146

The things they do are risky, sensationalist; they show they're not afraid and are willing to do anything. I'm not saying that what we're doing is good, I'm only saying that these guys have managed to bring down apparently untouchable people in just a matter of hours. So I think they are the way to bring down Castian Warnes. We owe it to the boss. Look what they've done to him. And I won't allow anything to happen to you – he would never forgive me. Are we good?'

'We're good.'

If Janina were a little older and had more experience, she would have realised that Candela's arguments don't stand up, but she is young. And Candela knows she can run rings round her. *I'm sorry, boss, I have to do it.*

The truth is that nobody knows who the Orwellians are. Candela has investigated them many times, but everything seems to lead to a dead end. There was a time when she thought they were a meme under which anonymous people claimed responsibility for their acts, something like the mask used by Anonymous. But their actions are very well co-ordinated. Someone leads them, and she is determined to reach that someone. She will get to them, and she will achieve her goal of destroying the Wanstein Club, even if it costs the last bit of innocence that Janina has left. She is sorry, so sorry for the girl, and she is sorry because she knows what that means.

'Candela, I'm going in. Watch out for me.'

Janina opens the door and sees a plaque nailed to a column. The plaque reads:

THE MINISTRY OF TRUTH

Behind all information is an opinion. It is impossible to inform without having an opinion. What is important is whether he who informs has the same opinion as you. The Ministry of Truth finds information that hides a different opinion from our truth and is, therefore, all lies. Truth is only a point of view.

She points the camera so that Candela can read it too. Outside this beam of light, everything is dark.

'Janina, look for a switch. We need more light.'

Turning the lights on, Janina sees a huge room full of columns, each about three metres high.

She does not know whether the camera gives Candela an idea of how enormous the place is, so she pushes everything she can out of the way, raises the camera as high as possible and films.

'It's immense. Go closer to one of the columns so that I can see exactly what it says.'

Janina does as she is told, going from column to column, showing the journalist first one, then the next, and the next...

'Candela, we have a problem!'

The ground has begun to shake. At first, she did not understand what was happening. It was like an earthquake. But then she realises that the column she had grabbed in her fright is slipping through her hands, sinking towards her feet.

'Candela, it's not the column that is going down, it's the floor that's rising! If it doesn't stop, the floor will rise up to the ceiling. I'll be crushed to death! I'm getting out of here!'

Just then, holding on to the column for dear life as the floor rises towards the ceiling, Janina hears the door she entered click shut and the lock turn twice.

TICK-TOCK TICK-TOCK TICK-TOCK TICK-TOCK

Continued on the following page >>

You haven't solved the puzzle on this page yet.
Find the code to work out where to continue reading.

If you need to, you can use the clues on page 166.

Write the code here so you can remember and refer to it later.

YOU HAVE SOLVED THE PUZZLE OF THE DOOR OF PLENTY

Continued from page 102.

Candela gives Janina the solution and watches carefully as the journalist enters the key.

Janina can hardly move her legs, the grain has reached her waist. She doesn't dare to think what will happen if the key turns out not to fit.

Click!

She pushes the door open and heaves herself into the next room. Some grain also pours through. There is dust from the husks everywhere. Her throat is dry, her nose blocked, and tears stream down her cheeks.

She has entered a kind of cave in which crystal-clear water runs down the walls. It's damp in here and it smells like a river. With all the cement tunnels she has come along, this seems like heaven. Janina is thirsty. As she points the camera all around the room for Candela to see, she goes up to one of the walls, her mouth open. She needs a long drink to slake her thirst.

'Oh no you don't, Janina! We don't know whether that water is safe to drink. Remember, anything could be a trap!'

'Do you think it's easy for me to forget that, Candela? Is that what you think?'

Thwarted, Janina washes her face and hands. She finds the canteen in her backpack and takes the three sips that she is allowed every three hours. Her food and drink are strictly rationed. Orders from Candela.

In the middle of the room stands a device whose purpose Janina cannot fathom. It is a transparent cylinder, about one metre in diameter, that runs from floor to ceiling, and from which a trickle of water flows. About halfway up the cylinder, at the height of Janina's chest, is a thin methacrylate plate that separates the water dripping down from the thick smoke that fills the section below. About five centimetres above this plate are a number of holes from which the accumulated water is leaking and, two centimetres above the holes, a slot which ends in something that looks like a conch protruding from the tube.

'What's that?'

'No idea, Janina.'

'Wait, Candela, there's something written here. I don't know if you can read it, the letters are transparent. I'll read it to you:

How much can a man with minimum support stand?

Suddenly, the water stops falling from the ceiling. A bell rings. As the water stops trickling down, the methacrylate plate, no longer held down by its weight, begins to rise until the holes are below it. Now, through the openings where water once dripped out, smoke begins to emerge.

Instinctively, Janina steps back.

'It smells of incense!'

'What?'

'It smells of church. Well, it makes sense, this is St Dunstan in the East.'

The fountain in the ceiling begins to flow again, and the water starts to accumulate in the cylinder once more. The methacrylate plate is pushed down, and no more smoke emerges.

'What's happening, Candela?'

'I don't know. Let me think…'

They are at the Ministry of Plenty. She needs to find a resemblance to present reality. Plenty, welfare state, consumerism. We need more and more things, because we create more and more needs: cars, technology, food products that come from the

154

other side of the world, clothing… We have to work harder and harder to pay for it all, and get into a vicious circle from which we can't emerge.

'Candela, the water has stopped again and the plate has risen…'

'Does it smell of incense again?'

'Yes.'

'OK, I'm on this. Stay calm and tell me when the water comes back again. And if you notice anything strange, let me know.'

'What do you mean, anything strange?'

Candela knows that the gas emerging from the fountain may not be harmless, but she can't tell Janina, not yet. She needs a few seconds to think it all through again. It was the poison gas in the Daedalus that left her in the state she is in now. She will never forget that. It got into her body without warning, being odourless, and destroyed it. *'Not, Janina, no… please,'* she thinks.

Taking a deep breath, she gets up from her chair and sits on the boss's bed. Her hands are shaking, so she takes his and squeezes them tight until she feels calmer again. 'I'll make them pay for what they did to you,' she promises. Her balance has returned to her once more.

She's been stuck like this for two minutes, with no clue how to get out. The stream of water from the ceiling stops increasingly often and, as a result, smoke keeps billowing into the room.

When Candela looks at the screen again, she notices that the camera is pointing up from the floor, as if Janina were sitting down.

'Janina, get up. You've got to get out of there! The smoke you say is incense is a narcotic gas. If we wait much longer, you'll fall asleep and you'll never get out, so get cracking. I want you to keep moving all the time now, OK?'

'Calm down, Candela, I'm fine.'

'You're not fine! Can't you see? You're too calm! We've got to stop the smoke coming out, find a way of stopping the lid from rising. I've got an idea.'

155

Candela instructs the girl to take out all the things in her backpack that can be used as containers, then fill them with the water that is falling down the walls and pour it into the conch over the holes.

The plan works. As long as the water stays at the right level, the lid does not rise and the gas does not come out.

'OK, now we've held them off for a while. Now we need to find out how to get out of this rat-trap,' says Candela.

'Don't mention rats! I told you I'm terrified of them!' Janina shouts furiously.

The flow of water from the ceiling is interrupted more and more often. Janina can't go on much longer – it's like trying to win a race in which your opponent never becomes tired but instead just runs ever faster. It's getting harder to keep the gas from escaping.

'Candela, I can't keep this up much longer! Some gas came out a moment ago because I couldn't get the water in quickly enough. Please hurry! I don't know how much longer I can keep this up!'

Janina pours more water in. But she is tired and stops for a moment, facing the walls where she is collecting the water. She looks down at the floor and, under the puddle that the water is forming as it falls, she sees something written:

In times of plenty, men fall asleep.

Candela copies the phrase under the previous one:

How much can a man with minimum support stand?
In times of plenty, men fall asleep.

She reads them aloud, thinking all the time. *The more we have, the more we want; the more we want, the more we have to work; and start again. Work, eat, sleep, work, eat, sleep...*

Candela repeats the two phrases aloud as she paces around the room like a caged animal.

How much can a man with minimum support stand?
In times of plenty, men fall asleep.
How much can a man with minimum support stand?
In times of plenty, men fall asleep.
How much can a man with minimum support stand?
In times of plenty, men fall asleep.

That's it! If you have just enough to survive, you fight to keep it. An endless circle. I give you a little, but I take away a lot; the less I give you, the more *you* need to give *me*. That is our society. That is the message.

'Janina, stop pouring water in.'

'What? But if I do that…'

It's OK, it's a trap. You won't be able to see the way out until you stop.'

'Are you sure?'

'You have to break the circle, Janina. Cover your nose, breathe in deeply and stop pouring water into the tube.'

Exhausted, Janina does as she is told. She breathes in deeply and stands still as the narcotic gas starts pouring out of the holes. The lid rises more and more. Then, below it, until now hidden by the smoke, several rectangles appear. Janina can't hold on any longer, and starts breathing again. When will the poisonous gas start to take effect?

TICK-TOCK TICK-TOCK TICK-TOCK TICK-TOCK

You haven't solved the puzzle on this page yet.
Find the code to work out where to continue reading.

If you need to, you can use the clues on page 166.

Write the code here so you can remember and refer to it later.

CLUES

Puzzle of the map (p. 8)
1. Remember you have a map.
2. Find the symbol that Candela saw on the map.
3. The symbol is not whole.
4. Look for the parts of the symbol and put them together like a jigsaw puzzle.
5. Once you have assembled the different pieces, you will see a number behind the symbol.

Puzzle of *1984* (p. 16)
1. Look carefully at the characters. They are not all numbers: there is a hidden phrase.
2. The characters form a cross.
3. Find this figure on the map.
4. The key is in one of the geometric figures.
5. Find the key in the cross made by the characters inside the geometric figure.

Puzzle of the Door of Truth (p. 24)
1. The text of the chapter contains crucial information.
2. In different parts of the text are references to the symbols that Janina sees, and to directions.
3. Start counting from the blue symbol.
4. Follow the path according to what the text says.
5. The number that the last symbol indicates is the key.

Puzzle of the Gate of Peace (p. 35)
1. The mirrors that divert the laser light are fastened with screws.
2. You found a screwdriver previously.
3. Use the screwdriver and change the direction of the laser.
4. Make the laser pass through the letters on the screwdriver.
5. On the map, find the figure you made by completing the previous operation.

Puzzle of the rails (p. 40)
1. Various images related to this puzzle appear in the text.

2. If you replace the question marks with letters, you get a phrase, which you need to decode.
3. The upper and lower white part forms several letters.
4. There are some equals symbols (=). Therefore, C = I and O = U.
5. This equation will enable you to decode the phrase.

Puzzle of Room 101 (p. 45)
1. Several cubes are hidden in the 101.
2. They are the same cubes that you have encountered in the book.
3. Each cube you found corresponds to a cube on the door.
4. The blue side indicates the key.
5. Note the symbol that corresponds to the blue side, and find it on the map.

Puzzle of the Ministry of Love (p. 56)
1. In the bottom part of the image the letters are in the wrong order. They say: 'YouTube: OK Go End Love'.
2. The text on the skull is the wrong way round, and we cannot read some parts of it, as they are under the drawing.
3. Find what the text on the skull says in the YouTube video.
4. Find the corresponding colours on the map.
5. Use the corresponding video to place them in order.

Puzzle of the Ministry of Peace (p. 62)
1. The text in the chapter tells you the amount of water you need to empty.
2. If there are 2,000 litres in each fish tank and you turn on the tap, how much water falls?
3. Not all the fish tanks are emptied. Take the communicating vessels into account.
4. Only half of some fish tanks are emptied.
5. On the map, find the code for the tap you need to turn on.

Puzzle of the first nexus (p. 69)
1. The numbers correspond to co-ordinates.
2. Read it backwards to get the results you need.

3. Enter the co-ordinates on Google Maps and use the Street View option.
4. Look around and try to find something that reminds you of the image in the puzzle. Don't forget to look up!
5. Find the symbols on the map.

Puzzle of John Milton's House (p. 76)
1. The image shows some blue lines.
2. If you place them on top of each other correctly, you will find a word.
3. If you know how the window opens, you know how to place the lines on top of each other and find a word.
4. The window opens upwards and conceals a six-letter word.
5. Find the word on the map to know where you need to go next.

Puzzle of the Path of Truth (p. 82)
1. There is something hidden in the image.
2. Try to see the whole image.
3. Look at the image formed by the black parts.
4. The black parts form a number.
5. The number has three digits.

Puzzle of the library (p. 89)
1. Look at the bookcase and the composition of the books.
2. A word is hidden among the shelves and the books. Look at the blue parts.
3. Some books have letters and numbers.
4. The word you found tells you the order of the letters.
5. The number that is left when the word is placed in order is crucial.

Puzzle of the Door of Plenty (p. 101)
1. We use glasses to see.
2. If you look through the stripes on a drawing of stripes, what happens?
3. Some stripes overlap, others cross each other.
4. If the direction of the stripes is the same, they are superimposed; on the other hand, the rest are erased and form a letter.

164

5. It should match the letter that you see with the letter on the glasses.

Puzzle of the trapdoor (p. 105)
1. It looks like a compass.
2. The text contains something more than it seems to say.
3. NO is really a symbol.
4. NO means northwest.
5. Look for northwest in the wind rose on the map.

The Goldstein puzzle (p. 112)
1. There are two white numbers and a white arrow.
2. The number 56 indicates the white arrow.
3. Column 5, row 6.
4. Below the pump are six pairs of numbers that lead to specific arrows.
5. Find the arrows on the map to find their values, and add them together.

Puzzle of the second nexus (p. 117)
1. The letters in the word *OyuUbet* are in the wrong order.
2. Look for *play* on the map.
3. Enter those letters on YouTube.
4. Follow the instructions on the video.
5. Find the word on the map.

Puzzle of the entrance to the Ministry of Truth (p. 123)
1. One part of the drawing turns. The other does not.
2. You need to know which sequence is the correct one.
3. You will find the sequence, in different parts, on the map.
4. Follow the correct sequence to read the letters below the numbers.
5. Find the word you make on the map.

Puzzle of the gravestone (p. 128)
1. There are some arrows on the gravestone.
2. Superimpose the grids as if you were folding the gravestone.

3. The lines overlap in some places. In others they form Xs.
4. All the Xs together form a word.
5. Find that word on the map.

Puzzle of the first step (p. 138)
1. The screws will give you the key.
2. Previously, you found an image containing those screws.
3. You will also find that type of screws on the map.
4. Put the plate with the screws and the map together.
5. You will find the key in the holes.

Puzzle of the third nexus (p. 143)
1. On the map there are some hexagons similar to those in the puzzle: they are examples.
2. If you discover the logic why each hexagon corresponds to each number, you will find the answer.
3. Something that is erased disappears.
4. Look at the shape that is left once the segments have been erased.
5. Each side of the hexagon corresponds to a number.

Puzzle of the Ministry of Truth (pp. 149–150)
1. There is something in the top section of the columns.
2. They are letters.
3. By assembling the Orwellian symbol, the columns are ordered correctly.
4. Ordering the columns also orders the letters.
5. The letters indicate a number.

Puzzle of the Ministry of Plenty (p. 158)
1. Some pieces are covered in smoke.
2. Place the numbers in their place and try to find the relationship between them.
3. From each two numbers another emerges.
4. Adding the first and the third numbers gives you the fifth. Adding the second and the fourth gives you the sixth.
5. The number that corresponds to the blue rectangle is the key.

166

SOLUTIONS

Puzzle of the map (p. 8)

The solution is: 78.

Puzzle of *1984* (p. 16)

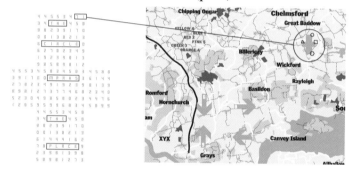

The solution is: 71.

Puzzle of the Door of Truth (p. 24)

The solution is: 145.

Puzzle of the Gate of Peace (p. 35)

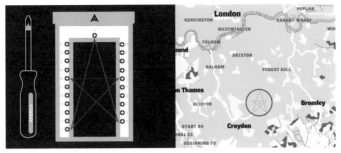

The solution is: 58.

Puzzle of the rails (p. 40)

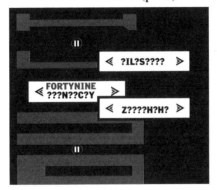

The solution is: 49.

Puzzle of Room 101 (p. 45)

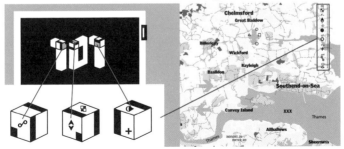

The solution is: 107.

Puzzle of the Ministry of Love (p. 56)

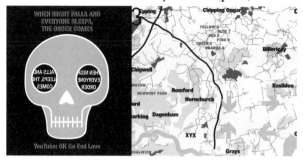

Two minutes and three seconds into the music video of 'End Love'
by OK Go, the members of the band come out of their sleeping bags:
the first is dressed in yellow; the next, in blue; the third, in red;
finally, the one dressed in pink emerges.

The solution is: 125.

Puzzle of the Ministry of Peace (p. 62)

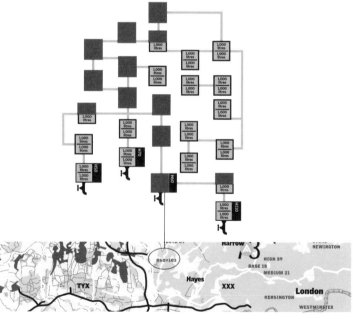

The solution is: 103.

170

Puzzle of the first nexus (p. 69)

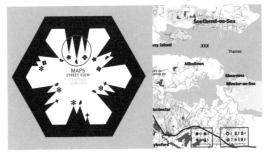

Google Maps Street View shows a tower with a silhouette

like that in the picture.

The solution is: 91.

Puzzle of John Milton's house (p. 76)

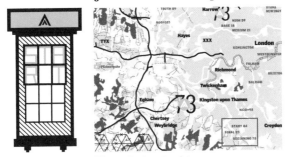

The solution is: 84.

Puzzle of the Path of Truth (p. 82)

The solution is: 130.

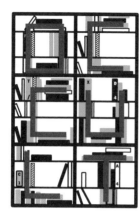

Puzzle of the library (p. 89)

The solution is: 119.

Puzzle of the Door of Plenty (p. 101)

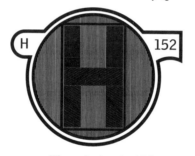

The solution is: 152.

Puzzle of the trapdoor (p. 105)

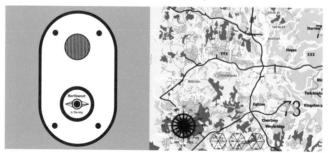

The solution is: 140.

172

Goldstein puzzle (p. 112)

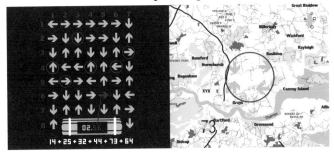

The solution is: 47.

Puzzle of the second nexus (p. 117)

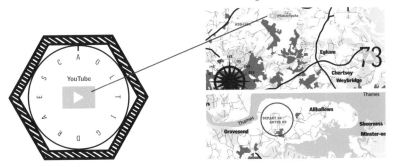

If you follow the YouTube tutorial, you obtain the word *exit*.

The solution is: 26.

Puzzle of the entrance to the Ministry of Truth (p. 123)

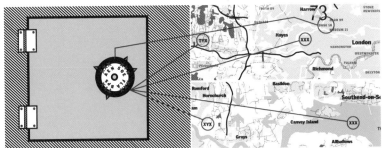

The solution is: 18.

Puzzle of the gravestone (p. 128)

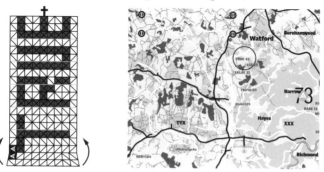

The solution is: 42.

Puzzle of the first step (p. 138)

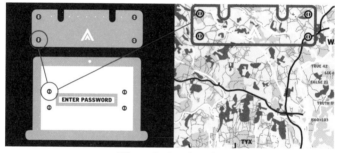

The solution is: 10.

Puzzle of the third nexus (p. 143)

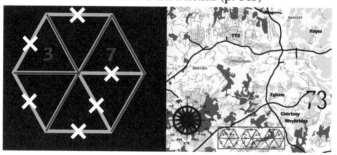

The solution is: 37.

174

Puzzle of the Ministry of Truth (pp. 149–150)

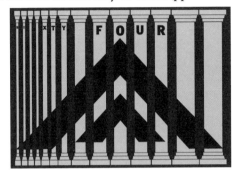

The solution is: 64.

Puzzle of the Ministry of Plenty (p. 158)

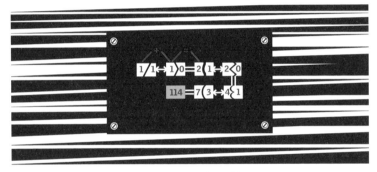

The solution is: 114.

73 Epping

Chipping Ong

YELLOW 0
BLUE 1
RED 2
PINK 5
GREEN 3
ORANGE 4

Chigwell

WALTHAMSTOW

Romford

NEWBURY PARK

Hornchurch

Ilford

STRATFORD

Barking   Dagenham

POPLAR

CANARY WHARF

XYX

WOOLWICH

Gray

IXTON

73 Dartford

FOREST HILL

Sidcup

Bromley

Orpington

ydon